Best wishes,
Roy Sheldon

THE CHICKEN COOP
CEO

 **FriesenPress**

Suite 300 - 990 Fort St
Victoria, BC, V8V 3K2
Canada

www.friesenpress.com

Copyright © 2017 by Roy Seidler
First Edition — 2017

All rights reserved.

No part of this publication may be reproduced in any form, or by any means, electronic or mechanical, including photocopying, recording, or any information browsing, storage, or retrieval system, without permission in writing from FriesenPress.

ISBN
978-1-5255-1093-9 (Hardcover)
978-1-5255-1094-6 (Paperback)
978-1-5255-1095-3 (eBook)

1. BUSINESS & ECONOMICS, LEADERSHIP

Distributed to the trade by The Ingram Book Company

THE CHICKEN COOP
CEO

Lessons in Life and Leadership

Roy Seidler

ROAR Leadership Consultants

Chicken Coop CEO – Lessons in Life and Leadership

I dedicate this book to my mother Margaret Winnifred Seidler who, with the most meagre resources, managed to raise eight children almost completely on her own.

Table of Contents

Part One – "My Story"
Lessons in Life and Two Crucibles 1

    Introduction to Part One   3

    Chapter 1 –
    The Early Years –
    "Rubbing up Against the World"   5

    Chapter 2 –
    The Value of Public Education
    and Crucible Number One   15

    Chapter 3 –
    Searching for Purpose   20

    Chapter 4 –
    Work History –
    Public Education 1974- 2008
    and Crucible Number Two   25

Part Two – Lessons in Leadership –
Intrapersonal Traits. 45

    Introduction to Part Two –
    Transitioning and Giving Back 2008 - TBD   47

    Chapter 5 –
    The "Inside-Out" Rule and the
    Importance of Emotional Intelligence   49

    Chapter 6 –
    Managing Ego and the Role of Humility   58

Chapter 7 –
Core Ethical Values that Drive Belief Systems 74

Chapter 8 –
Happiness and Subjective Well-Being 78

Part Three – Lessons in Leadership –
Interpersonal Skills 95

Introduction to Part Three 97

Chapter 9 – Employee Supervision –
Evaluation, and Discipline 99

Chapter 10 –
Decision Making 113

Chapter 11 –
Dealing with Change 122

Chapter 12 –
Time Management 129

Chapter 13 –
Planning and the Importance of Vision 138

Epilogue –
My Story Revisited: Poverty,
Continuous Learning, and Purpose 145

Endnotes 151

Acknowledgements 153

PART ONE – "MY STORY"
Lessons in Life and Two Crucibles

Pastor Ralph,

You can have the ~~Springfield~~ Transcona to keep.

Springfield book. Pink cover

The other ~~is~~ book is ● to read. I babysat him and 2 brothers & 1 sister. I was only 16 at the time. God Bless Margaret

INTRODUCTION TO PART ONE

In his book, *True North*, Bill George researched the life of many successful leaders. His research method was remarkably simple yet very effective. He asked the leaders to tell their life story. That was it. The leaders he interviewed consistently said that they found their motivation by understanding their own life stories. What he found was that most successful leaders go through three phases in their development.

The first phase, roughly birth to age 30, was labelled ***preparing for leadership***, or "rubbing up against the world." The second phase, between 30 and 60 years of age was labelled ***leading***, and the third phase, between 60 and 90 years of age, ***giving back***.[1] He found a common theme in the second phase, ***leading***. The majority of the leaders somewhere in the 30 to 60 years of age phase of their lives experienced something he called a "crucible." He defined a crucible as an experience that tests leaders to their limits. It can be triggered by a challenging issue at work or losing your job. It may also result from a painful personal experience such as the death of a loved one or a divorce. We all have had or will have crucibles in both our personal and public lives. My Grandmother Nina Gosselin used to tell me that if you start thinking too much of yourself, you will be "knocked down a peg or two." How we deal with our crucibles makes all the difference.

Some leaders in George's study suffered through illness, loss of position and even bankruptcy. This loss caused them to reassess what was truly

---

1   *True North*, Bill George, Warren Bennis Books, 2007, P. 16

important in their lives. What values and principles ought to drive their actions? In other words, what was their "True North?" Many of these leaders rebounded and came back stronger than ever having learned from the emotional impact of their crucible.

I perceive my leadership life to have followed this pattern. I have experienced the "rubbing up against the world" phase, the work-related crucible of phase two, and without sounding arrogant, I hope, in this last phase of my life, that I do indeed have something to give back.

When we tell our story, we accomplish two things. We understand ourselves better and without thinking too much of ourselves, offer support to people going through the same experiences that we did. Never be afraid to tell you story.

CHAPTER 1 –
The Early Years –
"Rubbing up Against the World"

Frank "Bud" Seidler - 1959

I must say, that for several reasons, records of the Seidler family tree are incomplete. What I do know is that my Grandfather, Jim Seidler, married my Grandmother (I never did learn her name) and they had my father, Frank Seidler, in Fertile, Saskatchewan. I am sure it is purely coincidental that Dad fathered eight children in a relatively short period and that he came from a place called Fertile.

Several memories of my childhood and two photographs stand out.

My father, Frank (aka Bud) Seidler, ended up in his childhood in the strange position of having both a stepmother and a stepfather. Dad and his mother left Saskatchewan and Jim Seidler in the early 1940's. They moved to Manitoba and my Grandmother married Tom Lesperance, the step father, who owned a saw mill seven miles east of Giroux. When my Grandmother suddenly passed away, Mr. Lesperance remarried a woman named Dorothy, who became my father's step mother. Dad also had two step brothers and two step sisters in this familial arrangement; talk about blended families.

> *Opposite is a picture taken in 1953 when we lived in Giroux next to the United Church.*
>
> *You can see from the picture that barber shop haircuts (that is me on the left) were not within budget. My brother Brian on the far right in the picture was still waiting for some hand me down shoes. I don't know what Linda was going to do because she had no shoes and there was no older sister! Mom looked good for having four children by her twenty-second birthday. Also, although I don't exactly recall the occasion for the picture, it must have been important because I was wearing my best pair of blue jeans.*

My dad had a lot of the emotional baggage that is often associated with broken homes and blended families. This impacted negatively on his ability, or in this case inability, to provide proper parenting. He was mostly absent when I was growing up.

My mother, Margaret, was born on February 3, 1930 to a young fifteen-year-old girl that gave her up for adoption. There were many theories about Mom's origins. Was she Icelandic? She had blond hair and blue eyes. We never did find out anything about her family tree.

She was adopted by Nina and Wilfred Gosselin. The Gosselins moved around a lot because Grandfather worked on the Canadian National Railway the went through the center of Giroux, a hamlet situated forty miles southeast of Winnipeg. My Mom and her family settled in Giroux for good in 1942 when my Mom turned twelve. She was allowed to quit school when she had completed Grade Six. At that time, Grandma Gosselin bought her some chickens to raise so she could make some money and have something to occupy her time. The job of caring for chickens was an interesting foreshadowing of things to come!

My Mom met my Dad when she was 17 years old and they got married on December 24, 1947. I was very precocious. I was born about seven months later, on August 8, 1948. Two years later, my brother Wayne was born July 3, 1950, followed by my sister Linda, born 13 months later, on August 23, 1951. My brother Brian, who died of pancreatic cancer at the age of 52, was born December 27, 1952.

After living in a converted granary and water house on the Lesperance farm for the first three of their marriage, my parents moved to Giroux. We lived in Giroux until I was seven years old. During that time, we lived in three different houses, two of which burned down, both under mysterious circumstances. Some found it curious that before the first blaze got going all the appliances and all our clothing were nicely piled on the front yard.

That first house was in the middle of renovations when it burned down. My Father had his best, possibly only steady job, working on the Canadian National Railway. He worked for the CNR for seven years. It was during this short period we were not very bad off. Dad had a job and meals were regular. The clothing budget obviously was not that flush but we did eat regularly and celebrated birthdays and Christmas with store bought gifts.

Giroux School # 1792: There were thousands of one room schools in Manitoba prior to consolidation in the 1960's, each with its own number. I point that out so no one will think that 1792, the number on the school, was not the year when I attended!

My Grade One Picture

I have vague but happy memories of those early years of my life. I remember that we were one of the first families in Giroux at that time that had a TV set; not everyone did in the early 1950's. I remember attending the one room Giroux School. There was a small library at the back of the school that to me was a magical place. It is strange how some aspects of my early life are so vague (supressed memories perhaps) and yet I have such a clear recollection of one of the first books I ever took from that library and read when I was in Grade One: Curious George. I fell in love with books and reading; a love that I cherish to this day. This was the only stage of my childhood, looking back now, that seemed "normal." That was going to change.

After the second house in Giroux that we lived in burned, my Dad obtained a ramshackle house that he could acquire for the cost of moving it. He intended to move it to a site later, carved out of the bush next to the one room Lorraine School east of Giroux. We spent over a year and one winter living in a converted chicken coop on the farm site of my Father's stepfather while we waited for the land to be cleared and the house to arrive. I remember that Dad had to nail up the little two-way flap doors the chickens had used to come in and out of the coop. There was no insulation in the walls. In the middle of the 300-square foot coop, my Dad hung a blanket to serve as a partition between the eating area and the sleeping area. There was no running water or plumbing; we carried our water in and our waste out! Wayne and I shared a bunk bed and took turns on winter nights lying next to the exterior of the coop. If you stayed in that positon too long, your long johns froze to the wall. Dad's work habits got more sporadic as did the regularity of trips to the grocery store. One of our main courses was venison which my Dad would shoot at any time during any season. The venison was a welcome addition to the meat staple we grew up with; bologna.

One of my most poignant memories of that winter was our "Christmas in the coop." There was no money for gifts, but we received a gift box donation from a local charity that contained an assortment of gift wrapped presents. I remember my brothers and sister and I going through the box and trying to sort out who would get what. I cannot remember any of the gifts, only that the charity was appreciated.

When we moved into the relocated house by the Lorraine School our life style grew more austere. My dad was most often gone. He was a construction worker in Alberta that first winter when we moved into the house next to the Lorraine School. My mother and I would cut enough firewood each evening to get us through the night and next day. We had to haul our water in a 5-gallon pail from the well-house on the school property. My brothers and sisters and I would go out foraging for wild fruit; I was particularly fond of wild raspberries. Wayne, being a bit of a "crack shot," would bag the occasional rabbit to supplement our protein intake. We were surviving day to day. I also had a job lighting the fire at the school each morning, but more about that later.

During the several years we lived by Lorraine School, Dad would come and go depending on where his construction work took him. He was gone more often than he was present during this time. While he was home, the family continued to grow. After a five-year respite from child rearing, four more siblings were born: Beverly born June 26, 1957, Russell born January 18, 1959, Garry born May 7, 1960 and finally the baby of the family, Darlene, born November 25, 1961.

In 1961, when I was 13, we moved to LaBroquerie where we lived for two years before moving once again, this time to Ste. Anne. We lived in a run-down rental home. I was now in Grade Seven and had started to become more socially aware of our poverty. Clothing was a problem. My mother would get credit at a local grocery store that allowed her to order clothing for us from the Sear's Catalogue; but with eight children to cloth, there wasn't a lot to go around. One of my most poignant memories of that first year in LaBroquerie was the first day of school in the fall of 1961. I did not have a pair of decent shoes. I did have a pair of rubber boots that were in respectable shape so my Mother insisted I wear them for the first day of school, until she could find something better for me. As fate would have it, we had just gone through a very dry spell, with no puddles to be found. I was in tears with embarrassment walking to school that day.

When I was 14 we were living in Ste. Anne. Dad's continued absences were of such a duration that my parents were in a state of pseudo separation. In fact, during this period he was even incarcerated for a time. We were told that his jail sentence was due to the fact he had several outstanding traffic tickets. I did not really believe that then, and I really don't believe it now. I never made a concerted effort to find the truth.

With my Dad now "out of the picture" and the lack of any income my Mother was forced to make a decision. We basically were living off handouts from the Grey Nuns. When the heat was cut off because the rent had not been paid for months, my Mom had no choice but to move. All eight of us were packed into a car and driven to my Grandparents in Giroux.

Roy and Wayne Seidler, 1964

Later that year, our parents signed off on a legal separation. A short time after that, my Mother moved to the city with the four youngest children and went on social assistance. My brothers Wayne and Brian and I and our sister, Linda remained in Giroux so we could continue our high school education in LaBroquerie. I moved in with my grandparents. My brothers Wayne and Brian and my sister Linda, lived with our Uncle Bob and Aunt Eleanor Burnell.

After being released from jail, my Dad moved out of the province to work in the construction industry in Alberta. I was to see him briefly only three more times in my life. My parents were officially divorced in 1970 and in 1977 we received notice that my father had perished in a house fire somewhere in Alberta.

One of the by-products of dealing with poverty was the development of a sense of humour (sometimes a little dark) to cope. My brother Wayne and I early on developed this skill, with Wayne clearly becoming the master. He had several jokes we used to poke fun at our poverty rather than wallow in self-pity:

- We were so poor, we couldn't pay attention.
- We were so poor we couldn't afford bowls, so we ate our soup out of low spots in the table.

- There were nine Seidlers in the family at one time, but Mom only had enough porridge for eight. Wayne claims this also accounted for our competitive nature on the baseball diamond. In truth, there were only eight little Seiders and they all survived to adulthood!

- We had a dog, but could not afford to feed him. Before he died he was so weak, we had to take him to the side of the road in a wheel barrow so he could bark at the cars. (No animal was hurt in the creation of this joke…we did not have a dog.)

While living with my grandparents, I attended high school in LaBroquerie. It was a difficult time for me. I felt the shame of coming from a broken home. I was poor, without the resources that were enjoyed by many of my classmates. I remember my Grandmother cutting down a pair of my Grandfather's pants for me to wear when I was in Grade Nine. They had big cuffs; not in style. While I am eternally grateful for the support and help my grandparents gave me, I never did get over having to wear those pants to school. Two years later, after I had my first regular job, I remember having enough money to buy my own clothes. I remember clearly that when I was fifteen years old, for the first time in my life everything I was wearing, shoes, socks, underwear, shirt, and jeans, were "store bought." The first time.

In reflecting on those early years the issue of poverty always comes to mind. Many people were poor in the late 40's and early 50's as the world put the Great Depression behind and emerged from four years of a terrible world war. I remember my Grandparents making comments about the "dirty 30's." My grandmother kept a large garden and canned and stored an enormous food supply in the basement. There was always the concern that the depression would return, so one had to be prepared.

It is hard for people today to understand the much lower standard of living that existed at that time. So, was it all bad? Is it possible that those of us who grew up in poverty inadvertently may have had an advantage? I don't recommend years of growing up in poverty and shame as the best course of action for character development but if you must live through what we did, you may as well learn and grow from it. It certainly provided me with the drive to want to overcome the poverty and succeed in later life.

CHAPTER 2 –
The Value of Public Education and Crucible Number One

In the mid sixties, the high school system was much different from what it is today. Like other school divisions in the province, Seine River School Division was very new. The consolidation of the one room schools into large centralized divisions had just taken place between 1959 and 1960. There were no guidance counsellors, library technicians or educational assistants. So, it was left to the principal to guide the graduating class.

> *The public-school system is the one social institution that can change the fortunes of a family in one generation.*

I am an ardent believer in and supporter of the public-school system. It has been said that the public-school system is the one social institution that can change the fortunes of a family in one generation. I knew this to be true because I lived that experience. I also believe that in the public-school system everyone is going to experience the support and guidance of a "significant influencer." For me that significant person was Mr. Albert Lepage.

I remember feeling quite proud of my accomplishment when I began Grade Nine in LaBroquerie. I had broken the record for the longevity of a Seidler in the public-school system. I remember thinking, as I was preparing to graduate, that I had set a record that would be hard to break. Little did I know what Mr. Albert Lepage, the school principal, had in store for me.

I always felt Mr. Lepage took a special interest in me. I was very impressed when he would give me the keys to his 1966 Pontiac car and ask me to go pick up the school mail at the local post office.

I remember clearly my interview with Mr. Lepage in the spring of 1967. He asked me what I planned to do after gradation. I told him I had a job waiting for me with a local construction company. He said, no, we are going to get you enrolled at the University of Winnipeg. I remember thinking why is he joking with me like this. I replied, "University is for rich kids and smart kids." Note the decided lack of self-confidence in my response.

He replied, "Well, I know you don't have the money, but you are smart enough. We will help you get the money you need." So, I did register. Mr. Lepage helped me get some bursaries and with the money I saved from my summer job, I paid my tuition fees in full. I was accepted to live in the men's residence, Room 302, Graham Hall. At that time, I had no vision of what was to come and I had no real belief that I could succeed. I was nearing my first significant crucible.

THE CHICKEN COOP CEO

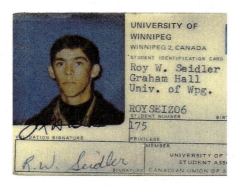

Look at that mug. One look says it all. I did not feel I belonged. U. of W. Student Card

I did not get off to a good start in my post secondary career. There were too many adjustments. I was lonely. I was failing academically. My level of commitment was not good. I couldn't wait to get out of the University and back to Giroux for the weekends. I had a cousin, Fred Champagne, who lived in Giroux but worked in Winnipeg. He would give me a ride out to Giroux on weekends and drive me back Monday mornings. By the end of October, I had had enough. I was going to quit. But, I remembered something Mr. Lepage had told me back in June. He had said, "Roy if you ever think you might want to quit, stop and see me first." I figured I would honour that request as I made ready to re-enter the building construction industry.

Mr. Lepage lived in a house on Rue Centrale in Ste. Anne, Manitoba. Ste. Anne was on the way from Winnipeg to Giroux on Highway 210. I asked Fred to stop outside Mr. Lepage's house. Since my drop in was unannounced, I didn't even know if Mr. Lepage would be home. I was secretly hoping he would not be home. I was very nervous about having to tell him I wanted to give up. Of course, he was at home.

I will forever remember most vividly Mr. Lepage's response when I told him about my decision to quit. He became quite agitated and questioned me about my decision. Once I explained why I wanted to quit, he responded, "Roy, I am very disappointed in you. With all your potential and all that we have done to get you enrolled, you are giving up too easily. You are better than that and you can succeed if you put your mind to it. I will tell you what: go back and give it another chance until Christmas. Then if you want to quit, go ahead, but don't bother stopping to tell me." Hello crucible number one.

LaBroquerie Collegiate Staff 1966 – Mr. Lepage sits in the middle.

I turned and left. I was flooded with a range of emotions: hurt, anger and self-pity. When I returned to the car in tears, Fred asked me what was wrong. I said, "Just shut up and drive."

Looking back years later I knew what Mr. Lepage had done. I believe he suspected all along that I would be challenged in the urban, university environment. He also took a calculated approach at that October Friday night meeting: some tough love. Here was a man that had come to know and understand me, who believed in me more than I did in myself. I believe his response was both calculated and caring. In the end, being a bit of a competitive person by nature, I said, "I am going to show him." I did return and made the Dean's Honour Roll in my first year.

Our recollections become our realities. My recollection, my reality is that Mr. Lepage made an enormous difference in my life. Not that I have anything against being a labourer in the construction industry, but Mr. Lepage's nudge got me going down a different career path. Years later I had the opportunity to meet and thank Mr. Lepage. I cried again.

I sometimes wonder how my life would have turned out if not for my first crucible and the intervention of Mr. Lepage. This type of reflection is what academics call, "counterfactual thinking." What would my life have been like had it not been for that pivotal event? What if on that October night I had not stopped on Rue Centrale in Ste. Anne to keep my promise with Mr. Lepage and share with him I intended to quit university? In my heart and mind, I know it was a good thing that I did stop. My life has turned out the better because of that decision.

The wonderful institution of public education had offered up two important concepts that would help define my future leadership beliefs and values: the "significant influencer" and the "crucible." In my life, there were more to follow.

CHAPTER 3 –
Searching for Purpose

Flash forward to November 8, 2016, when I was returning from the Elkhorn Resort in Clear Lake, Manitoba. I had just spent two very rewarding days conducting a leadership summit with the Central Office Administration and Principals of a North-Western school division.

As I travelled back down Highway 10 north of Minnedosa a curious thought entered my mind. For the first time since I was 14 years old, I did not have a job waiting for me somewhere, even while attending university. When I retired (or as I like to say, "transitioned") from the role of CEO of Seine River in August of 2003 along with my partner, Odette Labossiere, we founded ROAR Leadership Consultants Inc. and immediately I had another contract waiting. I signed a contract to become the Executive Director of the Manitoba Association of School Business Officials on September 1 of the same year. It has been a good run.

My First "Job"

If you define a job as something that involves a job description and pay, I would say that my first job was back to when I attended Grade 5 at the one room Lorraine School in the late 1950's. I was ten years old and had been hired by the local Board of Trustees to light the fire in the school's wood burning stove each morning at 7:00 A.M. during the winter months. This was to ensure that the building would be heated for the arrival of the teacher and the students later that morning. This clearly was before any work alone or any workplace safety and health regulations were in place not to mention child labour laws. I wasn't even old enough by today's standards to baby sit, and I was experimenting with the most highly combustible materials I could find to get the dang fire going each morning!

There were no safe work procedures in place nor was I provided with any training. My only support was a box of Eddy Matches. I remember many mornings when, due to wet kindling or matches, I was not able to get the fire going. I would have to retreat to our home adjoining the school yard to get my Mom to come back and help me. Somehow, we always got the fire going without ever having set fire to the school.

The pay was .50 cents a day (about $15.00 a month). I don't ever remember getting my hands on any of that money as meagre an amount that it was. My siblings and I were hoping to buy a hockey board game with the money. Somehow Dad collected my earnings for me and assured me he would take care of it. We never did get the hockey board game. I suspected at the time that the Hotel owner in LaBroquerie ended up with my earnings.

I got my second job when I was 14 years old while staying with my Grandparents in Giroux. My Mom had moved to the city by then. I was to be paid $3.00 a day by a local grain and hay farmer by the name of Doug Baird. Doug had a history of hiring teenagers from the town of Giroux to assist him with his field work. I was one in the line of many who had taken this position. Before school was out in the spring and again in the fall, I would work evenings after school and Saturdays. During the summer holidays, I worked 10-12 hours a day six days a week. This continued for four years until I graduated from high school.

I vividly remember my first day on the job. It was a cold wet day in mid April 1962. It had drizzled and snowed the whole day. It was too wet to work in the fields so Doug had me making trips into the woods near his farm to haul out firewood with a tractor and trailer. I had never driven a tractor before, but he gave me a ten-minute lesson and off I went on my own. The seeds of the joys of a low supervision work environment were sown. I started at 8:00 AM and worked to 6:00 PM with an hour off for lunch in the farm house. This was the longest and hardest day's work I had ever put in. When I got back home to Giroux, I was cold and wet. I had supper, took a hot bath and, exhausted, went right to bed and slept for 12 hours.

Doug was a benevolent fellow. Although the deal was I would get $3.00 a day, I was paid $21.00 a week. He explained that even though I did not have to report to work on Sunday, I would be paid for the day. Unlike the paycheque from lighting the school fires, I saw some returns from my labours. I turned the money over to my Grandparents who banked it for me. I accessed it for school supplies and clothing. I even bought a new bicycle (my first ever) the summer I turned fifteen so that I could cycle rather than walk the one mile to work each day from Giroux to Doug's farm south of town.

Reminiscing about those summers working on the farm, I remember indulging in frequent bouts of self-pity. Most of the other teens around town at the age of fourteen and fifteen did not have full time summer jobs. Often when I would be working in Doug's garden on a calm and warm summer day, I could hear the voices of children laughing and playing in Giroux. Some days I desperately wanted to be back in Giroux at the ball diamond with my friends rather than working on Doug's farm. I got over it. And the money was good.

Like growing up in poverty, working hard to get ahead was a character builder! I really do believe in the Nietzsche adage, "That which does not kill us makes us stronger."

My next foray into the job market was a summer job with Harper Construction during the years I attended the University of Winnipeg. Gordon Hornan, a local foreman with the Harper Construction Company, hired me and another young man from Giroux, Ernie Champagne to work for the company. The first summer we were employed we worked on a crew that was building the Central Grain

Facility in St. Boniface. Specifically, we were "cribbing." This is the process by which grain elevators were built back then. The main activity was driving large spikes through 2" by 6" planks, one on top of the other. It took two weeks for my hands to callous up enough so they didn't bleed each day. We were paid the minimum wage at the time of $2.10 an hour. Now the money was really rolling in; this amounted to double the daily pay I was making as a farm hand.

After graduating from University, getting married and having our first son, Stacey, I worked for two years as a postal clerk in Steinbach. I remember the annual salary being $6,600 a year as I worked as a letter sorter. I was working on what was called a "swing shift," which I now would describe as cruel and unusual! I would work one week of evenings, 4:00 PM to midnight. The next week would be the night shift, midnight to 8:00 AM. Then the "swing shift." This would be a combination of two evening and three night shifts. I am not sure if this type of shift work would be legal in 2017. It did terrible things to the biological clock. I also understand that the associated sleep deprivation component of this scheduling arrangement has been found to be advantageous as an interrogation method for breaking suspected terrorists.

The work was repetitive and monotonous. My co-worker, Lloyd Barkman and I would find ways to make the night shift more interesting, like racing letter "binnies" down the back corridor of the post office. One night, in the heat of the race, I failed to negotiate a corner and made a large hole in the wall. That one was a little hard to explain to our supervisor when he arrived the next morning.

On another occasion, during a night shift, we were playing hide and seek. Our work for the night was all done! I was hiding in an overhead locker and Lloyd had not found me yet. Just then, I heard someone enter the office. It was one of our supervisors, Brian Reimer, who had popped in to see how we were doing. He opened the locker where I was hiding. He just shook his head, turned, and left the office. We took hide and seek out of our extra curricular repertoire from then on.

While I was earning a comfortable salary, you can probably surmise from the two stories above that I was not a fully engaged employee. I was being called towards something that I had thought about a lot since graduating from university – teaching. I wanted to go back to school to get my teaching degree.

It was a giant step, but my wife Michelle was very supportive and agreed to take a job so that I could go back to university. At that time a one year post baccalaureate teaching degree was still being offered and off I went. It was a challenging winter for me and the family, but we persevered. Our son, Stacey was already born by this time. Two more wonderful children would follow, Kurt and Natalie.

Two months after graduating with my teaching certificate I returned to my high school roots. My leadership journey was just beginning.

CHAPTER 4 -
Work History – Public Education 1974- 2008 and Crucible Number Two

My view of success in life has been heavily influenced by the writing of Victor E. Frankl, the renowned psychiatrist who endured years of subhuman conditions in Nazi death camps and survived. In his book, *Man's Search for Meaning*, he had this to say about success: *"Don't aim at success- the more you aim at it and make it a target, the more you are going to miss it. For success like happiness, cannot be pursued; it must ensue, and it only does so as the unintended side-effect of one's personal dedication to a cause greater than oneself or as the by-product of one's surrender to a person other than oneself."*[1]

I have nothing against postal clerks; I was one. It paid well and was a secure job for a young couple with a young child. But I longed for something different. I had been inspired by Mr. Lepage and wondered if I could ever come close to finding the purpose in life of helping others as he had helped me. I sought out teaching to explore that calling. This was to become a theme in my 35-year career in public education and the work with ROAR Leadership Consultants Inc. since 2008. I believe success ensues. I am not saying we should not have career goals. The question is: are those goals consistent with the search for purpose and meaning in your life?

I remember a young teacher who made an appointment to meet with me when I was the Superintendent/CEO of Seine River School

Division. He would have been in his early twenties, in the "rubbing up against the world" phase, as described by Bill George. He asked me what he had to do to become a school principal in this division. I asked him what he was doing right now; it was a rhetorical question to which I knew the answer, and he told me. He was a physical education teacher in one of our schools. My advice to him was to go back to that school, concentrate on being the best physical education teacher he could be, be of service to his students, and see what comes of it. He went on to be one of our most competent and popular physical education teachers in the Division. He never did actively pursue an administrative position.

In addition to the "success ensues" mentality that I adopted, I also believe that I have been very lucky in my career. I have often been the right person, in the right place at the right time. Just lucky! A friend of mine once asked me why I thought I was lucky. That was a good question. Why do some of us seem to be consistently lucky while others would tell you that they can not buy a break? In a scientific sense, there is no such thing as luck. I think the difference is that I choose to believe I am lucky. Deep down, at some point in my life I started to expect good things to happen. When we have a positive outlook on life, we are more apt to recognize an opportunity and act on it.

Classroom Teacher 1973 - 1978

Luck was in full bloom four months after I received my teaching diploma in the spring of 1973. LaBroquerie High School, the very school that had launched my high school academic career, was looking for a junior high teacher. I had an interview with the principal, Mr. Hubert Bouchard who had been my Grade 10 Geography teacher at that school. The fit must have been good because I was offered the position before I left the interview room. My teaching career was underway; I became a classroom teacher until 1979, when good fortune again came my way.

Teacher/Principal 1979 – 1984

During the years between 1970 and 1978, the developing history of second language instruction in Manitoba conspired to provide me with my first positon in school administration. Here is the history.

Language is a nonmaterial human right to be valued. When Manitoba entered Confederation in 1870, the majority of the provincial population were French speakers, primarily of Metis heritage. Twenty years later, by 1891, French speakers compromised less than 10% of the population. Several provincial linguistic policies were enacted that further threatened the survival of the French language. French was abolished in the Legislature and in the courts in 1890 and then in schools in 1916. This contributed to the decline of public French usage in Manitoba.

When two languages are in close contact the minority language suffers. Assimilation into the majority culture, in this case English, with the loss of language tends to ensue. The Francophone community was getting increasingly alarmed with this trend. The citizens of LaBroquerie, being a particularly proud and strong Francophone community, were looking to reverse the assimilation trend. Successive provincial governments had been working towards a solution for quite a while.

Around 1947, Manitoba authorized the teaching of French as a foreign language in secondary schools. In 1955, the Liberal government under Premier Douglas Campbell allowed the teaching of French in Grades 4 through 6. French was gradually regaining its rightful place in Manitoba's education system.

This process continued in 1959 when the Department of Education approved a list of textbooks in French. A major victory was realized in 1967 when the government of Duff Roblin authorized the use of French as the language of instruction for other subjects, for up to half of the school day. Finally, in 1970, the Edward Schreyer government made French a language of instruction on an equal footing with the English. In 1975, to support the development of education in French, the Bureau de l'Education francaise was established and in 1976, the position of the Deputy Minister for French Education was created.

In the mid 1970's both the English and Francaise programs were being offered in LaBroquerie in the same buildings and under one administration. Officials of the Seine River School Division and concerned Francophone parents proposed the separation of the two programs, creating a K – 12 Francaise school and a K- 9 English Program school, each with its own separate staff and administration. The grade 10 -12 English Program students would be bussed to the neighbouring community of Ste. Anne for their final three high school years. While there was considerable dissent from both English and Francophone parents, the decision was taken to move forward.

> *It had not been that long ago I was living in a chicken coop.*

So, with the creation of a new K-9 English school in LaBroquerie a part time principal was required. With only five years of teaching experience, it did not occur to me that I should be interested. However, some of my colleagues in the school approached me and suggested that I apply. I had flashbacks to my famous interview with Mr. Lepage in that same building; my first crucible and the inspiration to strive harder. I was thinking even though I now had some money, I still felt insecure and unqualified for an administrative position. It had not been that long ago I was living in a chicken coop. Some of the stigma of the inferiority that comes with poverty remained.

Once again, I decided to acknowledge the confidence others had in me and applied for the position. I was successful. Education administration career, ready or not, here I come!

The administration time allotted to the position was not overly generous. There were 110 students in the school and I was given a .25

administration/.75 teaching position. I didn't know any better. I was healthy and had lots of energy so I made it work. The most interesting part of my new position was the principal's office I inherited. It was the same principal's office that was occupied by Albert Lepage when he had counselled me as a student back in 1967. My life had come full circle. Would I be able to live up to the same high standards that I had witnessed in Mr. Lepage?

> *If you can survive a winter in a chicken coop, completing an annual school plan shouldn't be that hard.*

When I think back on the experience of a first-time school principal, I realize now that I survived primarily on what I would call emotional intelligences while making a lot of basic organizational leadership mistakes. I provide by example my first ever "Annual School Plan." At that time, Seine River School Division used a business sector Management by Objective (MBO) approach to planning. Principals were required to determine improvement objectives, develop an action plan, and indicate how they would measure to determine if the objectives were met. I saw this as a pen and paper exercise to meet an external requirement. I completed the form on my own in my office. If you can survive a winter in a chicken coop, completing an annual school plan shouldn't be that hard.

I choose only those objectives that I knew I could achieve and would be measurable. For example, because LaBroquerie Elementary was a new school, we had to establish a library. I choose the objective of increasing the number of books by 20% a year. Guess what. We did, and I could measure that.

I had devised another less measurable objective: develop a homework diary for students to complete and have signed by their parents each night. I was proud of that one. Less measurable but measurable none-the-less and thought it would be helpful. I did not consult teachers or parents. I thought this was how someone should lead. When I asked the president of the parent council what he thought of the diary, he commented, "it is a waste of paper." I did not include his comment in my measurement of success. I got some great feedback on my plan from the Assistant-Superintendent. From what he could see, I was doing a great job getting the new school up and running.

Looking back, I feel embarrassed about my early leadership naivete. But back then, I led the way I had seen others lead. The duty culture was still strong. I ran a school that emphasized positive feeling tone, a term I had picked up at a workshop. At that time, I had no formal leadership preparation and received little or no on the job training.

My greatest supports were the principal of the K-8 francophone school, Ecole St. Joachim, Mr. Gilles Normandeau and the principal of the Grade 9-12 francophone high school, Mr. Rino Ouellet. They both had previous administrative experience and I learned the power of networking. We held monthly lunch meetings to coordinate the activities in our respective schools. We called the meetings "SNO" for Seidler, Normandeau and Ouellet. You should be careful with acronyms. Someone commented we were trying to "snow" people.

President of the Seine River Teachers' Association (1983-1984)

With 5 years of teaching experience and 4 years of part time administration experience, I was encouraged to run for the Presidency of the local Teachers Association. Should I succeed, I knew that this would be a leadership opportunity on a different level; my first leadership opportunity outside the safe and collegial atmosphere of our little school.

I was running against a teacher from one of the larger schools in the division and someone who had been involved in the Teachers' Association for quite some time. He was very popular with many teachers. I had two year's experience on the Divisional Teachers' Association Board as a school representative, and in my own mind, I was the underdog in the race. While my confidence as a school leader was growing, I admit to feeling frightened by the challenge that would come with being the leader of representatives from every school in the Division. Because there was an administrative component to my teaching duties, I was looked upon with suspicion by some teachers. Whose interests did I have in mind? There was a concern that as a member of the Principals' Association, I might have split loyalties. There is an old saying, be careful what you ask for…. you might get it. I won the election.

> *I felt that I had fooled people into thinking I was more competent and talented than I was.*

I must admit that initially, I felt I did not belong as the leader of that group. I felt that I had fooled people into thinking I was more competent and talented than I was. I have since learned that there is a name for this feeling: the "imposter syndrome."[2] I remember the frightening, dry mouth feeling I experienced when I had to chair the first meeting of the association. I was experiencing performance anxiety. It is hard to have a presence when you think you are an imposter!

When you feel like an imposter, we don't give ourselves enough credit for the internal strength and skills that we possess. We tend to see ourselves as the beneficiary of undeserving good fortune; and we become afraid that we will be found out. While this mindset might help keep us humble, a good thing, too much of the syndrome can hold us back. While I felt I had advanced a long way up the social ladder since my chicken coop days, there yet lingered pangs of low self-esteem. I am also an introvert by nature; and that didn't help. When would I be able to stop worrying that I had to prove myself and to others that I was a capable and worthy person, and not an imposter?

During that year as President, I began to develop some strategies that helped me gain more confidence. I started to reflect on purpose…a theme that would grow stronger as my career progressed. I started to remind myself that the role of the President of the Association was not to be a self-serving career move. It was an opportunity to work in a larger professional circle to improve the outcomes for our students. That mindset, that sense of serving a purpose other than myself, gave me courage. It still does today any time my consultant work takes me back into the public education system.

Acting Assistant Superintendent 1985

In October of 1984, the Superintendent of Seine River School Division resigned. The Assistant-Superintendent at the time, Mr. Jean Suszko, was appointed Acting Superintendent for the remainder of the school year while the Board conducted a search for a new Superintendent/CEO. In October of 1984, Jean and the Secretary-Treasurer, Mr. Andre Chaput drove from the Board office in Ste. Anne, picked me up at my school in LaBroquerie and took me out for lunch. During lunch, they asked me if I would be interested in the position of Acting Assistant Superintendent for the spring term, 1985. I did not see that one coming. Because I was promised the opportunity to return to my school in LaBroquerie for the next school year, I agreed.

I felt I was a very lucky person. This leadership opportunity was not something that I was actively pursuing; nor was I fully confident that I had the capacity to perform the required duties of that position.

That six-month, term position experience was very valuable in expanding my leadership knowledge and my understanding of how larger systems work. I received some on the job mentoring from both Jean and Andre. They helped me understand larger system functioning. For instance, I was given an active role in helping develop the Board's annual budget. I began to understand the concept of the "local and the remote." As a school principal, I understood how my school functioned, but did not fully appreciate how my school was only one of fifteen in the division. I remember when principals would get together they would often express doubt and suspicion of the intentions of the Board and the Superintendent's office. Those bodies were perceived as "remote" and consequently were not necessarily to be trusted. Now, I was part of the "remote." This inherent mistrust of remote authority was another lesson that would help me as my career progressed.

Both Jean and Andre helped me understand the critical role played by an elected school board in providing the direction for the school division. They also helped me understand and appreciate the importance of developing and maintaining a healthy and trusting working relationship with the Board. This was knowledge and experience that would serve me well in the future.

Principal Dawson Trail School 1985 – 1989 and a Mini-Crucible

As the 1985 school year wound down I was completing my interim Acting Assistant Superintendent position and preparing to go back to the familiarity and safety of my small school, LaBroquerie Elementary. Little did I know that the Superintendent and the Board had something else in mind for me.

Dawson Trail School in Lorette, Manitoba, was a dual track English – French Immersion school with 450 students that was considerably larger than LaBroquerie Elementary that had just over 100 students in a single-track setting. The principal at that school was retiring in June and so the administrative position at that school was open. It was a full time administrative position with a part time vice-principal.

I am not really into conspiracy theories, but I often wonder about what happened next. Was there a succession board somewhere in the division office with pegs representing people that got moved around from time to time? If there was, my peg was not going back into the hole designated for LaBroquerie Elementary. That is where I wanted to go, but the Superintendent informed me that I needed a greater growth opportunity. I got it.

> *I am not really into conspiracy theories, but I often wonder about what happened next. Was there a succession board somewhere in the division office with pegs representing people that got moved around from time to time?*

When I arrived at Dawson Trail School I assumed that the culture and the norms for working together at that school would be similar or the same to LaBroquerie Elementary and that my bag of leadership tricks would work just as well. Wrong.

One of the first duties I undertook, thankfully before the first school plan had to be created, was to prepare a teacher/student handbook to share at the annual fall meet the teacher night. I got it ready and had the school secretary run off the required number of copies. The next morning the Vice-Principal, Gerry Thiessen, came into my office. She closed the door and threw a copy of the handbook on my desk and said, "Roy, what the hell is this?" She went on to say that important documents such as this were created and reviewed by the staff in a collaborative fashion. Collaboration. My vision of leadership was expanding. I call this a mini-crucible. It did not become major crucible because I had the good sense to realize that Gerry was right. I was not respecting the norms in that school. She was right and by acknowledging my error, I was able to develop an excellent working relationship with Gerry, not to mention a lot of good coaching!

My school planning process would improve over my first amateur attempts back at LaBroquerie. That first year at Dawson Trail, the school plan, developed in the spring, was a collaborative effort with all staff involved. I introduced a forced prioritization process that resulted in school goals that had a chance to make improvements in student learning. We even got feedback from parents. I was starting to feel confident about myself as a leader. I wish I had remembered my Grandmother's admonition that, "if you start thinking too much of yourself, you will be knocked down a peg or two." I was about to get knocked down a considerable number of pegs, not on the succession board, but with my ego.

Ste. Anne School 1989 – 1991 and Crucible Number Two

The 1988-1989 school year was a difficult one for Ste. Anne School. Ste. Anne School was a complex, large K-12 English Program school of about 300 students. It was a regional school that received high school students who had graduated from K-8 schools in smaller surrounding communities. It shared a large building complex with two other schools: a French Immersion Program School and a Francaise Program School. Each of these schools had its own separate administration and staff.

The principal of Ste. Anne School became ill and had to leave in the spring of 1989. An acting-principal was named to finish the year.

Someone again was playing with my peg on the succession board at the division office. That someone, the Superintendent I assume, thought my peg would fit very well into the hole for the Ste. Anne School principalship that was now empty. I did not want to go. This probably contributed to crucible number two that was lurking around the periphery of my career. I had only been at Dawson Trail School for four years and was just hitting my stride.

Mr. Suszko, the Assistant-Superintendent, took me out for lunch again. I should have been nervous. He was a very persuasive fellow and I know that he had the best interests of Ste. Anne School and my career on his mind. He felt that I would be a good fit for that school: right person, right place, and the right time. I took the challenge.

> *My existing array of administrative leadership strategies as I entered this new position was going to be tested in ways that I could not have imagined.*

For a variety of reasons, I will not dwell on, the culture in the school was not good; the morale of staff and students was low. There was a lot of confrontational issues with parents. This was a very different environment than I had experienced in my previous two schools. There were cliques on staff. The fact that this was a K-12 school that shared a complex physical facility with two other schools clearly was a factor in setting the tone in the building. There was a lot of competition rather than cooperation for issues such as space, entrances and so on. My existing array of administrative leadership strategies as I entered this new position was going to be tested in ways that I could not have imagined.

I am going to detail one issue regarding my leadership role at Ste. Ann School and how I dealt with it, because it provided the most significant professional leadership crucible that I had ever experienced. That issue concerned the manner that the high school programming was scheduled.

The ***traditional scheduling model*** for high schools was the one I had experienced as a student back in the 1960's. There were 8 periods a day with a class change and a new subject approximately every 40 minutes. This scheduling remained constant for the entire year. In the late 1980's and early 1990's an alternative model became popular. It was called the ***block scheduling model***. There were variations on this model but the most significant difference was that instead of 8 x forty minute classes a day there 4 x eighty minute classes a day. This model has also been referred to as the ***semester model***. For one half the year a student would study only four subjects rather than 8 and four more in the second half the year or semester. Ste. Anne Collegiate was on the block scheduling/semester system.

There were three English high schools in Seine River School Division at that time. One of them was on the semester system and the other was on the traditional or annual system. The principal of the school that followed the annual system was a friend of mine and I was influenced by his example. I was also biased by the fact that an 8-period day was what I was familiar with. Other than having been a high school student I had little experience teaching at the high school level and none at the administrative level.

In the fall of my second year at the school, I presented the high school staff with my belief that it would be in the best interests of our students to move to annual system. I believed that. The resistance was immediate and strong against the idea. Models of change theory popped into my mind. My response was, "lets take a professional approach and take a few months to review the research, visit other schools and gather any other data relevant to the decision on the table." Everyone was pleased with this approach; it looked like a serious exercise in consensus decision making. Since the staff had challenged me on a few other ideas that I had floated, I too was happy with this approach.

The months flew by and at each staff meeting we would dedicate time to discussing what we were finding regarding the annual versus the semester system. We were finding that both the research studies and the personal examples that were shared with us were evenly split as to the merits of each system. You could find research that would support either model and point out the deficiencies in the other.

> *There was a lot of "confirmation bias" taking place and I was as guilty of that as anybody.*

There was a lot of confirmation bias taking place and I was as guilty of that as anybody. It was not until years later that I became familiar with that term. Confirmation bias happens when someone is only willing to consider information and data that support his/her position and excludes everything else. We were all looking for evidence to support the belief we currently held.

Somewhere around mid-March decision time had come. If we were to make changes for the next year we needed lead in time. At a staff meeting, we took a straw vote, hardly a consensus building way to end the dialogue and debate. The majority of the teachers wanted to stay with the block/semester system. Two teachers abstained. No one spoke in favour of moving to the 8-period annual system. Since I have already given you a heads up about an eminent crucible, I would give odds that you already know what happened next.

Although I had given the staff every indication we were in a consensus decision making mode for the last several months, I made an administrative, command decision and at the next meeting announced we would be moving to the annual system. I got the School Board approval to proceed. For a staff that already suffered from lack of morale this decision was not going to help. The staff was ready to revolt.

> *To this day, when I share this story in public, and I do, I blush with embarrassment. I had been rocked to my core. What happened?*

Another consequence of moving to the annual system resulted in a reduction of preparation or non-contact time for the high school teachers on staff. This in turn resulted in the local teachers' association filing a grievance with the School Board. The high school teachers did not agree with the reduction in their non-contact time that resulted with the introduction of the annual system.

To this day, when I share this story in public, and I do, I blush with embarrassment. I had been rocked to my core. What happened?

When I was not able to convince the staff to move to an annual scheduling system based on my **personal authority**, my character, and my competence as an educational leader, I invoked my **positional authority** as principal of the school and commanded it. It was Michael Fullan who said you can not command that which matters the most. I should have listened.

There is a time for the command mode. Winston Churchill was an excellent war time leader because the times called for a decisive command leadership style. He did not succeed as well with his leadership approach in times of peace. There are also times when a leader needs to invoke the command style as a form of moral outrage; a time when there is such an obvious and grievous transgression that the leader must call someone on it. The decision to move to an annual system did not call for a command decision, we were not at war, nor was it a matter of moral outrage.

Even if I had been nominally right about the benefits of making the change, and as I have pointed out the research was not clear, I exercised poor judgement in forcing it on the staff. I should have been the bigger person and backed off. I guarantee the staff would have demonstrated an increased vigor in their teaching to prove that they were right about the semester system. The students would have been the biggest winners of all.

I got myself into this crucible because I was not clear enough about my own beliefs and values, about my understanding of leadership styles, about team building and about life in general. I had never been challenged like this. It was at that time, when I felt so threatened that I seriously considered quitting, that I picked up Stephen Covey's book, *The Seven Habits of Highly Effective People*. When the student is ready, the teacher will appear. I was ready and Covey's book introduced me to **principle based leadership.** It led me to reflect on my core beliefs and values in a way I had never attempted before.

One of my favourite quotes is by the former British Prime Minister, James Callaghan:

"In my judgement, a leader should have some core philosophy and belief against which he can judge the important issues as they arise. Unless he has the bedrock to fall back on, the unexpected storms that blow up will toss him about like a cork. Without such a foundation, a leader may be able to survive, but he won't be a leader in the sense that I use the term."

I did not want to be a cork. I began work on a personal mission statement that helped me clarify who I was and what I wanted to become. I had relied too much on the advice and the leadership approaches that seemed to work for others and never seriously said, "Hey, Roy: what are your core ethical values and what is your leadership model? What will work for you? What do you believe?" To err or fail is not tragic. Failing to learn and grow from your experience is the tragedy. We will not live long enough to learn from our own mistakes. Edwin Land, the American Scientist and inventor, who invented the Polaroid Camera, once commented, "A failure is a circumstance not yet fully turned to your advantage." He got the picture!

We can learn from our own mistakes and failures and those of others. I hope you never live through the mistake that I made and that you can avoid doing so by learning from my lapse in judgement and its consequences.

While all this was happening at Ste. Anne School, someone again was playing with my succession plan peg at the Board office just across the street from the school.

THE CHICKEN COOP CEO

Assistant Superintendent 1991 – 1995

Early in 1991 the Superintendent of Seine River School Division retired and Mr. Suszko was appointed the new Superintendent. A consulting firm was hired to conduct a search for a new Assistant-Superintendent to fill Mr. Suszko's soon to be vacated position. Given my recent personal challenges in school administration at Ste. Anne School, I was somewhat surprised when I was approached and encouraged to apply by some of my colleagues in administration. Understandably there was quite a bit of interest in the position within the division. There were two factors in my favour. I had the previous experience of the Acting Assistant back in 1985 and I was functionally bilingual, a requirement for the position.

I remember clearly the one on one interview I had with the consultant company representative. It lasted an hour and half. What I remember was the expert interviewer got me speaking about my beliefs and values. This exercise was fresh in my mind. I did not know if I would make the short list to be interviewed by the Board of Trustees, but I felt good about having had the opportunity to talk to someone about my career.

> *I pitched a good game. We won. What else had I won that day?*

I did make the shortlist of four candidates recommended by the consulting firm to be interviewed by the Board. There were ten trustees, a consulting firm representative, the Superintendent, Secretary-Treasurer, and Assistant Superintendent in attendance. Quite a crowd, and somewhat intimidating. The interview was late on a Friday afternoon. After the interview, I left and drove to Dugald, Manitoba. I was the starting pitcher for the Giroux Athletics versus the Springfield Chiefs that evening. I pitched a good game. We won. What else had I won that day?

> *While I would not be seated in the chair of the CEO, I had made it to the Board Room. It was about the same size as a chicken coop.*

A month later, around 8:00 AM, I was sitting in the Principal's office at Ste. Anne School getting ready to walk the halls and greet students and staff as they entered the building. I was surprised when the Superintendent arrived. He had news for me. The Board of Trustees at a regularly scheduled meeting the night before had voted to appoint me as the new Assistant-Superintendent to begin duties August 1, 1991. While I would not be seated in the chair of the CEO, I had made it to the Board Room. It was about the same size as a chicken coop.

The five years I spent in my new position were the most professionally satisfying of my career, certainly to that point. The new Superintendent, Mr. Suszko, allowed me a great deal of autonomy and encouraged high levels of initiative. I found this to be very motivational and I wanted to do a good job; to be worthy of the confidence he held in me.

About six months into my job, someone asked me how I was handling the stress of my new position compared to being a school principal. The person was surprised when I responded that the stress was different, and not as great. I was not tied to the rigorous 9:00 AM to 3:30 PM routine of the principal. Unless you have been a school principal, it is hard to understand the constant demands on your time and energy. While the hours I spent in my role as the Assistant were more than when I was a principal, there was less urgency in my work. I had time to plan and meet with people. While there was a great deal of responsibility that came with the position, it was a much different type of stress.

Superintendent/CEO 1995 - 2008

In the fall of 1994, Superintendent Suszko informed the Board that he would be retiring at the end of the current school year. There was one more jump for my peg waiting to be effected on the succession planning board in Seine River School Division.

Early in the spring term of 1995, once again, I was asked to go out for an evening diner by someone from the Board office. It wasn't Mr. Suszko this time. It was the Board Chair, Mrs. Wendy Bloomfield and the Vice-Chair, Mr. Marinus Van Osche. I wasn't as nervous this time.

Having already passed the scrutiny of a consulting firm to enter central administration in the Division, I was considered a good option to fill the position of Superintendent of Seine River School Division. They asked me if I would consider an appointment as the Superintendent to replace Mr. Suszko. I felt I was ready for this final step in my professional career. I accepted the offer.

I remember the night of my appointment. There were a lot of thoughts and emotions going through my mind. I recall being in tears as I drove home that night after the appointment. Flashbacks to poverty and chicken coops raced through my mind. I was a lifer in SRSD. My connection started as a student when the Division was originally created on April 1, 1959. Now the Board had given me yet another opportunity to continue to develop my leadership skills.

My fourteen years as Superintendent/CEO was the longest duration of any of the positions I held in Seine River School Division. The Boards I worked for were very supportive of and invested in my growth as a leader. For this I will always be grateful. It helped get me through Bill George's second leadership phase of leading and hopefully has prepared and has enabled me to give back and share what I have learned as I progressed from a chicken coop to a boardroom.

Final Comments on Part One

As mentioned earlier, I have been lucky in life. I have had the opportunity and support to learn and grow in my career in the Seine River School Division. I have had the support of family, friends and two "significant influencers." I have made the study of the role of the leader a passion in my life.

So, what have I learned and how have I grown? As I live out the final stages of my leadership journey, what do I have that I can give back? This is what I shall share in Part Two and Part Three.

PART TWO – LESSONS IN
Leadership –
Intrapersonal Traits

INTRODUCTION TO PART TWO –
Transitioning and Giving Back 2008 - TBD

There are no short cuts to wisdom. We are not born wise. We can speed up the acquisition of knowledge, but knowledge itself does not make us wise. When we gain knowledge, we learn. But again, learning is not wisdom unless we start to apply the knowledge and learning to our personal growth. The variables of time and experience are critical in gaining wisdom.

In his book, *Outliers*, Malcolm Gladwell introduced the world to the "10,000-hour rule":

> "*The idea that excellence at performing a complex task requires a critical minimum level of practice surfaces again and again in studies of expertise. In fact, researchers have settled on what they believe is the magic number for true expertise: 10,000 hours.*"[3]

ROAR Leadership Library - Giroux

I began writing this book over two years ago; I have been preparing to write it for 40 years.

I have a personal library in our home office that contains over 250 books that deal with the topic of leadership. I have read them all. Over my 40 plus year career, I have attended numerous conferences and workshops on the topic of leadership. More importantly, I have had the opportunity in my own leadership role to apply the knowledge I have gained. This is when the true growth occurs. Hopefully, and I will leave that to others to judge, this is when wisdom starts to set in. I don't know if I have the 10,000 hours yet to become an expert on the topic of leadership, but I must be close! However, even falling short of being able to consider myself expert, there are some beliefs I have about great leaders that I am comfortable sharing with others.

CHAPTER 5 –
The "Inside-Out" Rule and the Importance of Emotional Intelligence

"This above all: to thine own self be true,
And it must follow, as the night the day,
Thou canst not then be false to any man."
– Hamlet Act 1, scene 3, 78 – 80

I have conducted numerous workshops dealing with leadership over the years. I always start with two questions and allow for some table talk for the workshop participants. The first thing I do is ask them to come up with a definition of a leader. How would you define the noun, leader?

Invariably, people come up with something like, "Someone who helps individuals and organization achieve their stated mission and goals." I happen to like this one: "Someone who seriously meddles in the lives of others, in a non-manipulative way." Great leaders make the world a better place. But how?

This leads me to the second question. I ask participants to think of three people they consider to be or to have been great leaders. It could be someone living or dead; someone they know personally or a historical figure. Then I ask them to list the character traits of those three individuals that they think so highly of as great leaders. Without exception, every time I have facilitated this activity the group comes up with something like this:

Intrapersonal Traits – Self Awareness – How We Manage Ourselves	Interpersonal Traits – Social Competence – How We Handle Relationships	Cognitive Skills - IQ
Optimistic	Empathetic	Knowledgeable
Trustworthy	Kind	"Well Read"
Integrity	Compassionate	Intelligent (IQ)
Self-confident	Good communicator/listener	
Conscientious	Service oriented	
Takes initiative	Fair	
Humble		
Inspirational		

After participants post their traits on the wall, I cluster them under these three categories. The first two columns, intrapersonal traits and interpersonal traits were one time referred to as "soft skills." In a ground-breaking book written by Daniel Goleman in 1998, we became familiar with the term "emotional intelligence." Goleman claimed in his book, *Working with Emotional Intelligences*, that one's intelligence as measured by one's intelligence quotient (IQ), "explains surprisingly little of achievement at work or in life."[4] Consistent with that comment is the fact that in the "great leader exercise," cognitive skills of the great leader were the least cited character trait of a great leader.

The first two columns above describe the qualities of emotional intelligence.

Goleman asserts that a person's success in a leadership position depends on three things: entry level expertise, IQ, and emotional intelligence. Not surprisingly he claims that for people in the highest levels of leadership and supervisory responsibility, "On average close to 90% of their success in leadership was attributable to emotional intelligence."[5]

In Seine River School Division, we thought enough of this exercise to make it a question when interviewing candidates for leadership positions in the division. If you ask an interviewee to give his or her theory on what constitutes great leadership, you normally get some sort of "canned" response; a short precis on the literature. But if you surprise the interviewee with the "three great leader question," the responses are much more telling about that candidate. They are not giving you theory, they are sharing something deeply important to them and that tends to be more useful in finding the right fit for a position.

When I awoke on June 20, 1995, the morning after the Board of Trustees appointed me the new Superintendent of Seine River School Division, two thoughts immediately ran through my mind. After the euphoria and congratulations of the night before, I looked into the mirror and said, "You accepted to do what?" The second thought that I had in the days, weeks, months, and years to follow was the day after my appointment, I suddenly did not get smarter!

While my intelligence quotient (IQ) stayed the same over night, I knew that my job description had changed dramatically and along with that came increased expectations and supervisory responsibility. What did I have to learn and how would I have to grow to meet those increased expectations?

> *While some people with excellent technical skills succeed when they move into more complex supervisory leadership positions, others fail, sometimes miserably.*

My entry level expertise to the position of school principal and later of CEO was that of a teacher. While some of my teaching skills were transferable, other skills were not yet developed. While some people with excellent technical skills succeed when they move into more complex supervisory leadership positions, others fail, sometimes miserably.

In my former role as Superintendent of Seine River School Division I had the privilege of working with members of our central office team who were able to develop and hone skills beyond their technical entry level expertise.

Paul Ilchena, the Secretary –Treasurer of Seine River School Division, is a qualified accountant. When he assumed his new role some of his technical entry level expertise was still required to oversee an annual $30M budget. But Paul also became a supervisor and leader of more than one hundred people, had to work directly with an elected Board of Trustees and had to deal with multiple issues involving all staff, parents, and tax payers.

Like me, he had to develop new skills and abilities to perform his duties as Secretary-Treasurer.

He relied less on his entry level expertise and intelligence quotient and more on his emotional intelligence.

Successful leaders demonstrate that who you are as a person is more important than your technical expertise, especially as you assume greater supervisory and leadership functions.

This is generally referred to as the **"inside-out"** concept. You cannot hope to succeed in leading others unless you can lead yourself. The emotional intelligences of self-awareness, self-confidence and self-motivation are critical.

This is why as the principal of Ste. Anne School I struggled in my leadership role. I was like the cork on the ocean. I had not done enough serious self-awareness deliberation nor had I clarified my core beliefs and values about leadership. I was too vested in trying to lead the way I thought someone else might and had not worked on my own intrapersonal traits.

In his book, *The Seven Habits of Highly Effective People*, Stephen R. Covey explains the importance of a leader gaining the trust of those around him. That trust is a result of the leader being a genuine person of integrity. You must start there. We need to have competence and expertise also, but without depth of character we will be limited in our leadership efforts.

The "Inside-Out" Trust Based Leadership Model

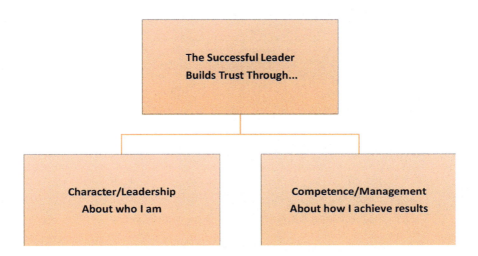

The good news is that while our IQ remains relatively constant throughout our lives, we can work on and improve our emotional quotient. The method of doing this is to practice self-awareness or awareness capturing. Being self-aware means that you can monitor your thinking and your emotions. It allows you to have a clear perception of your personality; your strengths and weaknesses. It helps you be aware of how you are reacting to other people, especially if you tend to get defensive too quickly.

> *It is sad and career threatening when you get offended easily when no offense was intended. It is even more career threatening when you get defensive when an offense was intended.*

We are three people: who we think we are; who other people think we are, and who we really are. Self-awareness helps us understand the first two of these definitions. By practicing self-awareness, you can make changes in the thoughts and interpretations you make in your mind. This in turn allows you to adjust your emotions. Self-awareness is one of the key emotional intelligences defined by Goleman and is the most critical factor in the "inside-out" concept in achieving success in life and leadership. It is sad and career threatening when you get offended easily when no offense was intended. It is even more career threatening when you get defensive when an offense was intended.

Final Word on "Leadership Models"

> *All models are wrong, but some are useful.*

My personal leadership model assumes we must have developed a good understanding of who we are as a person before we can succeed in leading others. Upon that foundation of personal self-knowledge, we develop trusting relationships with others because of our character and our competence. However, as confident I am of those factors, I close this chapter with some advice: all models are wrong, but some are useful, and when it comes to leadership models, there are no silver bullets. You must find what works for you.

Jean Chastel, a French farmer and inn-keeper, was credited with killing the beast of Gevaudan on June 19, 1767 at Mont Mouchet France.[6] The beast entered future literature as a werewolf that had been terrorizing his friends and neighbours by tearing out their throats. Apparently, the beast could not be slain by normal methods. Jean, however, used a "magical" silver bullet made from a medal representing the Virgin Mary and blessed by a priest to kill the beast.

The silver bullet metaphor came to symbolize a magical solution to an extreme or complicated problem. It reminds me of the adage that for every complicated problem there is a simple answer; and it is always the wrong one. So, it is with leadership models.

There are many "leadership models": principle based leadership, servant leadership, transformational leadership, charismatic leadership, participatory leadership, situational leadership and so on. What is a leader to do? All models are wrong, but some are useful. No one model can hope to capture all the intricacies of the human psyche and the myriad of leadership contexts and challenges. Leaders need to be cautioned against identifying too closely with any given leadership model in the literature, especially if they start to get the sense that it is not working for them.

I remember as a School Principal and later as an Assistant-Superintendent I had the opportunity to observe a variety of leadership styles in the Superintendents of the Seine River School Division. In total, I observed five Superintendents, each with his own unique leadership style. One was a very articulate philosopher type, one was a sharp-witted man with a great sense of humour, one was an excellent model for the importance of continuous growth, one was the charismatic strong leader type, and one was a man passionate about public education but had a reputation of, "don't mess with me."

In my first year as the new Superintendent in 1995, I had to deal with a discipline issue with an employee. Without going into the details of the infraction, and there had been an infraction, I decided I would deal with it the way one of my former Superintendent mentors would have dealt with it: the "don't mess with me" approach. While it worked for my former mentor, it was a disastrous approach for me. I ignored my somatic marker. A somatic marker is a term coined by neuroscientist Antonio Damasio for the sensations we experience in our body that tell us, if we are sensitive enough, when a choice feels very wrong.[7] I invoked a very direct strategic temper tantrum approach. I knew immediately that the "don't mess with me" demeanor that I adopted was wrong for me and I regretted it later. While my direct approach, that lacked in empathy for the individual, resolved the situation in the short term, I had damaged my long-term relationship with the employee. I went for a short-term win-lose approach rather than taking more time with the individual and trying to reach a win-win resolution.

As a Superintendent/CEO, I often took the advantage of my positional authority to exercise my belief that a leader should also be a teacher and a presenter. I would take the opportunity in school principals' meetings and retreats to share with our administrative team the gems I had gleaned from my most recent workshop or a book that I had read.

I was somewhat taken aback after one such session when one of the principals, approached me and said, "Roy, I don't care what those *otters* say (sic – he meant authors – he was a Quebecois with a strong accent and had trouble with his "t's" and "h's" in English), I want to know what you think." Ouch. Mini-crucible #2. His name was Simon Laplante and he was one of the administrators who could care less about my positional title. His strong suit was honesty and I appreciated that. I took two positive lessons from that exchange. Number one, he saw me as approachable enough to be able to share what he thought. Number two, he was right. What did I think and what were my personal values and beliefs? I needed to do a better job of articulating that.

> *Unless you are going out werewolf hunting, remember, forget the "silver bullet" approach when it comes to adopting a leadership style.*

The lesson here is while you are honing your leadership skills, be aware of the leadership literature. Take into consideration lessons learned from your mentors. But in the end, listen to your own "somatic marker"; trust your instincts and be true to your core ethical values. Unless you are going out werewolf hunting, remember, there is no silver bullet when it comes to leadership style. There is no magical model that you can adopt. There is only one you!

Chapter Five Key Takeaways

- The inside-out concept: Before we can succeed as leaders we need to self-reflect and be clear about the beliefs and values that drive our actions.

- More than entry level expertise and IQ, emotional intelligences are the key to leadership success.

- Leaders become trustworthy when they combine good character with managerial competence.

- There is no "magic bullet": discover your own leadership model.

CHAPTER 6 –
Managing Ego and the Role of Humility

"Time wounds all heels."
– Groucho Marx

When people get into positions of greater supervisory authority and decision making responsibility, they start to change. It might be subtle at first. However, no matter how much we want to think we are being humble and practicing good self-awareness, gradually we start to think a little more of ourselves than is helpful.

Robert Sutton wrote a very insightful book, dealing with jerks in the workplace called, *The No Asshole Rule*. I highly recommend it, even if you don't think you have an ego problem. He summarizes the issue of "ego creep" very nicely in his book:

> "Leaders of most organizations not only get paid more than others, they also enjoy constant deference and false flattery. A huge body of research – hundreds of studies – shows that when people are put into positions of power, they start talking more, taking what they want for themselves, ignoring what other people say or want, ignoring how less powerful people react to their behaviour, acting more rudely, and generally treating any situation or person as a means for satisfying their own needs – and that being put in positions of power blinds them to the fact they are acting like jerks."[8]

Not a pretty picture!

It is good to be self-confident and decisive, but when we start to think that we are infallible and that others are there only to serve us, we have a problem.

Another activity that I facilitate in leadership workshops is one that explores the role of "ego" in defining leadership success. The instructions are simple. I ask the participants to jot down the first three things that enter their mind when they think of the word, ego. When I chart the responses, they can be grouped into two columns: positive and negative connotations of the word. At a recent workshop, I conducted, this is what was shared:

Ego - Liability	Ego - Asset
Thinks a lot of themselves	Confident
Always right	Strength
Misuse of power	Sense of self
Boastful	Assertive
Lack of assertiveness	
Loud	
Overbearing	
Need for reality check	
Demanding	
Time consuming	

The results above are typical of the responses I get when I facilitate this exercise. Ego is not inherently a negative or a positive attribute. But it tells you something about the reality that many people have had to experience with a leader who exhibited qualities listed in the first column where ego is a liability rather than an asset. People don't leave their jobs, they leave their bosses.

> *Personal authority is derived from the positive character attributes of the leader; the most important being a sense of humility.*

Leaders possess two kinds of authority: positional and personal. Positional is the title the leader is given: supervisor, manager, department head, CEO. Personal authority can be exercised without even having a title. Personal authority is derived from the positive character attributes of the leader; the most important being a sense of humility.

The Importance of Humility

I remember my first day on the job as a principal in 1979. I stood proudly at the front door welcoming students on the first day of school. One student, Sheldon, a kindergarten student, was suffering from a severe case of school anxiety. Apparently, he also had overeaten his morning allotment of oatmeal. The result was a large regurgitation of said oatmeal just inside the school entrance. There was no custodian on duty at that time. So, off I went for the mop pail. My first official "positional" duty as a school principal was to clean up some vomit. Someone was blessing me early in my career about the importance of being humble. Thank you, Sheldon.

Later, when I was a beginning CEO I had another similar reminder of the insignificance of positional authority and the importance of being humble. As a Superintendent/CEO I asked to be invited to visit classrooms. On this occasion, early in the school year of 1996 I was invited to sit in on a Grade 1 class. The teacher was generally considered to be the most competent of early years' teachers. Upon entering the classroom, the amount of preparation and organization of the teacher for the day's lesson was apparent. There was going to be some activity based learning.

Manitoba is a province that rightfully values the inclusion of all students in the regular classroom. In this classroom was a special needs student named Jason. He suffered from fetal alcohol syndrome and was known to exhibit periodic outbreaks of disruptive behaviour. Jason had a full time educational assistant assigned to him to help him manage his behaviour. As so happened, Jason was about to have a bad day. About 10 minutes into the lesson it was obvious Jason was not going to hold it all together. He began running about the classroom, throwing books and at one time tried an after-touchdown conversion with the garbage can. Poor teacher!

Both the teacher and the EA began the process of cornering Jason. When they did so, it happened right in front of me as I sat off in a corner to observe the lesson. He had calmed down somewhat, and the teacher commented that he had better behave and asked him if he knew who I was. He did not. She told him he better behave because I was the division Superintendent. To that Jason responded, "I don't give a shit." Positional authority in some situations is irrelevant. It is good for our humility to be reminded from time to time. Thank you, Jason.

> *"Seidler, what the hell is wrong with you? Were you sitting on your brains this morning? The damn busses should not have been on the road."*

On yet another occasion, towards the end of my CEO career, in grips of a significant snow fall and high winds, we decided to let the school busses run. Around 10:00 AM I received a call from what sounded like a young male caller. He asked, "Seidler, what the hell is wrong with you? Were you sitting on your brains this morning? The damn busses should not be on the road." Then he hung up. In times of inclement weather, when we cancel school, I would normally get a few calls critiquing the decision. In times of inclement weather, when schools remain open, I would normally get a few calls critiquing the decision. You can't win! Part of the job. I would always try to explain politely the rationales for the decision. One thing I did learn, shutting down the bus runs and closing the schools was always well received by students.

Later that morning I got a call from one of our high school principals. He informed me that a grade twelve student, Kenneth, was going around the school sharing with his classmates that he had called Seidler and given him a piece of his mind. The principal asked me how I wanted to handle the situation. I told him to commend Kenneth for taking the initiative to make his opinion known. I could see some leadership ability in this young man. Also, I asked the principal to advise him to watch his language the next time he called the Superintendent. Thank you, Kenneth.

Successful leaders can manage their ego. In his book, *Good to Great*, [9]Jim Collins defines the top leaders in the companies he studied as people who were humble but driven, with an emphasis on humble. When things went right they gave credit to others. When things went wrong, they took personal responsibility; they never said, "The problem is out there."

I have known CEO's who have worked with a Board they did not agree with. When that becomes the case, as a leader, you need to make some decisions. One, do you gripe and criticize the Board members behind their backs or do you take the opportunity to exercise your abilities to help the Board grow? Remember, the problem is never out there. What are you going to do about it? Talking about people behind their back will not help the situation. If you are not man or woman enough to do something about a dysfunctional situation, then you are probably not the right person for that job.

> *A strong sense of humility helps people control ego and achieve personal authority to complement positional authority.*

A strong sense of humility helps people control ego and achieve personal authority to complement positional authority. These people realize it is their example and their modelling that gives them true authority, not their title. I always tried to take the view that the employees in the division were not there to serve me, but rather I was there to serve them; how can I help them do their jobs. This servant leadership approach is difficult to invoke when we play our ego on the liability side.

A leader with a balanced ego takes a positive view of the world. Where others see problems, they see opportunities for learning and personal growth. Because they have self-confidence, they are more inclined to give up the need to defend and so are more competent in dealing with difficult interpersonal relationships.

Finding the right balance of just enough ego is key. For instance, I always considered myself a very loyal person and I certainly was a loyal employee of SRSD. But at some point, I had to realize that too much loyalty can become an ego problem. When we are too loyal we run the risk of being blind to weaknesses and problems. People will not want to give you the bad news along with the good.

> *No matter how humble we may think we are, leaders can start to take things for granted and start adopting an air of entitlement.*

No matter how humble we may think we are, leaders can start to take things for granted and start adopting an air of entitlement. Is it inevitable? I believe it is.

When I first became the Superintendent of SRSD, a friend of mine said, "People will start treating you differently." I did not want to believe that but there was some truth in it. As a CEO, some people will want to cater to your every whim, possibly to win favour. So, what happens after a while, if we are not careful, we start believing in our own infallibility, thus weakening your judgement and effectiveness.

I remember my last day on the job in SRSD. It was in August of 2008. I had been an employee of Seine River School Division for 35 years. When I left the division office that day for the final time and headed to my car, I carried a small cardboard box of personal belongings: some pictures I had on my desk, personal copies of some treasured leadership books and that was it. The realization set in that the other objects in my office, the support I had from an excellent administrative assistant, technology support, the salary and benefits.... all those things...came with the position not the person. They were now going to support the next person in that position. Humbling indeed!

The Curse of Getting Defensive

One of the signs that our ego has become a liability is when we get defensive. By practicing self-awareness, and accepting the feedback of others, I realized long ago that getting defensive has been a weakness for me. I often have wondered if my need to be defensive found its origins in the insecurity that I harboured because of the poverty and shame I experienced in my youth? When I was younger I did not make the distinction between being defensive as an emotional reaction to a perceived threat and defending an idea. These are two different mindsets; the former negative, the latter positive when exercised appropriately.

The path to getting defensive usually starts with an action, comment or even something as simple as a raised eyebrow of another person. We pay attention to what happened. We process what happened, make an interpretation in our mind, feel an emotion and then react. It is what happens between the initial observation and the reaction that ensues that is important. If only we could slow down time. We can have mature, professional reactions or we can get defensive and act like a child. This natural tendency to get defensive is deeply rooted in our DNA.

Our ancient cave man ancestors had three main drivers of their behaviour: looking to eat something, avoiding being eaten by something and procreating. Upon seeing a sabre tooth tiger approaching, there was little or no time to process thoughts. The autonomic defensive mechanisms kicked in, pumping chemicals into the blood stream that gave them immediate heightened physical strength to run like hell or stand and fight for their life. In avoiding being eaten they often employed what we would now call a "limbic highjack." Limbic highjacking, also known as emotional highjacking, occurs when our amygdala releases brain chemicals that create fear and anger. Our cognitive, rational thinking is by passed. After having experienced extreme cases of this state of being, some people literally can not remember what happened to them.

The most common version of this fight or flight phenomenon today is road rage.

> *Unless I am mistaken, not too many CEO's are being threatened by sabre tooth tigers in the Board office these days.*

Unless I am mistaken, not too many CEO's are being threatened by sabre tooth tigers in the Board office these days. However, the ancient part of our brain sometimes still interprets the actions of another in that manner and we adopt a severe defensive stance and lash out. Not good. Our judgement and decision making gets compromised. I can remember with regret the times after a meeting when I choose to react in a defensive posture. I believe in the adage, "three times a day leave something unsaid." There were times when I had surpassed my three times a day limit before noon.

Over time I learned seven strategies that helped me stave off a defensive posture after an unpleasant interaction.

1. Practice awareness capturing. The elevated heart rate, the blushing around the neck and the narrowing of peripheral vision (good for avoiding sabre tooth tigers) were sure signs I was losing it. Time to leave something unsaid.

2. Seek first to understand then to be understood, a mindset made popular by Stephen R. Covey.

3. Replace judgement with compassion. When you understand why someone else might be having an off day, it is easier to suspend judgement and not rush to defensiveness.

4. Use the "balcony view." Visualize yourself objectively stepping out of the situation and adopting the stance of an external viewer.

5. Practice active listening: this really helps when you are seeking to understand.

6. Don't take it personally.

7. When confronted by someone aggressively trying to get you upset and hence defensive, silently think to yourself, "I have a list of three people that can get my goat. You are not on it!"

How did some of these principles assist me reduce the urge to get defensive?

During the week of August 12-16, 2002, I was away from the office attending the annual Superintendents' Leadership Summit at the Gull Harbour Resort. When I got back to my office on August 19, I had several voice mails, two of which grabbed my immediate attention.

Before I get to the voicemails, allow me to provide some background detail to the subject of those calls.

In 2002 in Manitoba parents had the right under provisions in the Public Schools Act to request that their child be accepted into a school other than their local community school, either another school in the division or another school outside the division. If the principal in the requested school had room to accommodate the student, the request could be granted. One of the difficulties with this arrangement was with transportation. School boards were not required to provide transportation for choice of school students. Some did and some did not. It was SRSD's policy to transport choice of school students who opted for another school in the division if there was room on an existing route that could accommodate the child.

In my absence during that week in August of 2002, a parent had requested that her son be accepted, under the provisions of the choice of schools' regulations, into a neighbouring divisional school for the upcoming school year. The request had been approved, but there was no existing bus route between the child's home and the new school to provide for his transportation. The Transportation Supervisor, correctly interpreting the Board Policy, had denied the request for transportation. The School Principal and the Secretary-Treasurer, in my absence, had already confirmed that bus transportation would not be provided. Trouble was brewing.

I call the narrative to follow the "Roy Snidler" story. When I had recorded my voice on the answering service, I had a cold. My enunciation must have been a little off, because the mother who called referred to me as Roy Snidler. Well, I hope it is because she did not hear my name correctly.

The first voice mail left on August 15 went like this: (Precise names of the schools and individuals involved have been changed.)

"Hello Roy Snidler. I have a son who is supposed to be going to the School "X" who your division sent a letter denying him transportation and I just want you to know that you will be picking my child up. You pick up other children in this area and you are denying my child access to school. I pay my taxes and we will be getting the local newspaper involved and we will be getting a lawyer because we are going to sue you for denying my child access to school.

> *So, he is either on the bus or you will be hearing from the local newspaper and our lawyer.*

So, he is either on the bus or you will be hearing from the local newspaper and our lawyer. So, I suggest you phone me back. I expect a phone call Monday because school starts in less than two weeks and I need to get my son to school and if you think I am driving every day you will be paying me for my vehicle maintenance and gas. So, you have a nice day!"

Since I had no access to voice mail, I had not responded to the parental call. Hence, the next day on August 16, the mother left another message.

"This is Mrs. X again and I just want to inform you there is a bus one-mile from here. It can turn in our driveway. We can drive a tractor and hayrack into our yard. It is three minutes tops for a bus to come in here. We are currently talking to the local newspaper. They are very interested in our story and our lawyer is talking about suing you. You have three options: pick up my child, cut my taxes or reimburse me for my wear and tear and gas.

The first option is you will be picking up my child. I just want to inform you of that. You better call me Monday because I will be calling you. It would be nice of you to call me first to show that you even give a shit. You have a nice day!"

I had been given an enormous break here. Between the initiating event, two aggressive calls from Mrs. X and my opportunity to respond, I had some time to reflect and plan. Had she reached me in person on one or both calls, I would like to think I would have responded calmly and professionally, but given my propensity to get defensive, I am not so sure!

I had time to plan and gather some information. Mrs. X's residence was over a mile, one way, off any existing route. She had been given the correct response to her request. I also contacted the community school her son had attended the previous year and found that there had been some negative interpersonal interactions between the mother and the principal of the school as well as some of the staff. Over the summer a new principal had been transferred to the school. As well, I learned that Mrs. X was a single mother who commuted to work in Winnipeg each day with limited ability to driver her son to school. By moving her son to a different school, she had set herself up for a very stressful situation. Replace judgement with compassion.

When I returned her call, the interaction **_could have gone_** like this:

RWS: "Hello Mrs. X. This is Roy Seidler returning your calls of last week. I understand you have some questions regarding our transportation policy?"

Mrs. X: "You are damn rights I have questions. My son needs transportation, I pay my taxes and you are going to get off your ass and get him to school on the bus next Tuesday."

RWS: "Excuse me, Mrs. X, but I don't appreciate your tone of voice."

Mrs. X: "Well that is too bad, because my taxes pay your wages and I want something done about my situation immediately. I am thoroughly ticked off by now!"

RWS: "I don't have to take this kind of abuse from you!

Mrs. X: "Then I guess I will be talking to my trustee, my lawyer and the local newspaper.

RWS: "Please call back when you want to be more respectful to me." And I hang up.

OK! Hold the phone! Can you imagine if in fact, with the time I had to prepare to return the call, to get the facts and brace myself, I still gave in to a limbic highjacking? There would not have been any, seeking first to understand, no replacing judgement with compassion and I certainly would have been taking the interaction personally in this hypothetical response. What I needed was a balcony view.

So, this is how the return call did go. (Actual transcript) It starts out the same, but this time RWS refrains from getting defensive!

RWS: "Hello Mrs. X. Let me begin by apologizing for not getting back to you sooner, but I was away at a conference last week. From your messages, I take it you have some questions regarding our transportation policies."

Mrs. X: "Your damn rights I have questions. My son needs transportation, I pay my taxes and you are going to get off your ass and get him on that bus next Tuesday.

(Note: this is where the facts begin to differ from the earlier defensive scenario above.)

RWS: "I can understand the stress you must be under with school only a few days away."

Mrs. X: "You got it. I don't understand why he can not be on the bus."

RWS: "Actually, I have reviewed the situation already and our transportation department people have given the correct interpretation of policy. As a choice of school parent, you are not eligible to receive transportation for your son. We have no busses in that area to accommodate your request."

Mrs. X: "I don't care about your damn policy, I have to get my son to school."

RWS: "Can we consider some other approaches to resolving your problem?"

Mrs. X: "Like what?"

RWS: "Would you consider leaving your child in your local community school?"

Mrs. X: "I have tried unsuccessfully to resolve my problems with the staff at that school."

RWS: "Are you aware that there is a new principal at your local school effective this year?"

Mrs. X: "No."

RWS: "Would you be prepared to receive a call from the new principal if I were to ask her to contact you? Possibly she could assist you with your unresolved concerns."

Mrs. X: "Ok, but if this doesn't work out, I want my son on the bus."

RWS: "Thank you for your willingness to speak to the new principal. Let me know how things work out."

You can probably surmise who I called next. I called the new principal and asked her to get in touch with Mrs. X and invite her to come to the school for a meeting.

Mrs. X did get the call. She did go for a meeting. Later that same day as chance would have it Mrs. X called me when I was out of the office. She left another voice mail.

Mrs. X: "Hi Mr. Seidler, this is Mrs. X calling (in a calm and pleasant voice, and she got my name right). I went to speak to the principal and the teacher and I was very impressed with the new principal and the teacher is the same thing, I was very impressed."

The teacher is willing to help my son. I found this principal to be much better. I feel that if I have a problem, I can go to speak to her any time. This is how I wish my experience would have been before. We had to fight for so much.

I appreciate your phone call today. Thank you very much for that! My son will be going to school with his sister.

Again, thank you so much. I appreciate it. Thank you and have a great day."

Do our interpersonal dilemmas always get resolved this nicely? Certainly, this one would not have if I had adopted a defensive stance as characterized in the first fictional scenario.

When I called Mrs. X I was prepared for some harsh words from a stressed-out parent: replace judgement with compassion. Seek first to understand. Consider a third alternative. This is all good theory. It is even better when it plays out successfully in the real world.

I would like to share one final story about the joys of resisting the temptation to get defensive. This is a shorter story.

Each fall school divisions in Manitoba are required to conduct public consultation meetings regarding their annual budgets. In the fall of my final year as a CEO I was attending such a meeting. A local municipal counsellor, lets call him Jack, approached me at a coffee break with concerns about the increase in spending that was being proposed in the budget. In Manitoba, local municipal counsellors must collect taxes as requested by the school board to balance its budget. Jack approached me rather aggressively, reminiscent of a saber tooth tiger. He commented that if the Board did not have to pay my six-figure salary, local taxes would be less. He went on to say that I was earning more than Buck Pierce, the quarterback for the Winnipeg Blue Bombers. Without an ounce of defensiveness in my posture, I replied: "Yes, Jack, but I had a better year." There was a long pause and then we both broke out in laughter.

Chapter 6 Key Takeaways

All leaders are in danger of "ego creep."

Great leaders manage their ego by practicing self-awareness and humility.

Positional authority is strengthened when a leader also possesses "personal authority."

Control the natural tendency to get defensive.

CHAPTER 7 –
Core Ethical Values that Drive Belief Systems

"When your values are clear to you, making decisions become easier."
— Roy Disney

Prior to 2003, numerous Adult Learning Centres were popping up around the province. There seemed to be a need for this service. They were established to improve the educational and employment prospects of adults who had dropped out of school early. By 2008 there were 7,929 registered adults attending Adult Learning Centres. In 2008 a graduating student commented: "For the last 49 years of my life I always wanted to get my Grade 12 diploma, and if it was not for the teachers and staff at the ALC, I would not have been able to achieve this goal."

The problem was that prior to 2003 there were no proper provincial guidelines in place for the establishment and operation of the ALC's. So, in July of 2003 the province passed the Adult Learning Centres Act. The government then began approaching individual school divisions which had an ALC within their boundaries and asked if they would be willing to assume the responsibility to administer the restructured ALC. Seine River School Division had one such ALC in Ste. Anne.

Suddenly the Board was tasked with a governance decision. What was there in our vision, mission beliefs and values that would guide the discussion and ultimately a decision?

The dialogue and debate started around the board table. Initially there was no consensus and if anything, as the CEO, I suspected that the Board would not want to take on this responsibility. There were concerns that there would be hidden costs even though the centres were to be fully funded by the province. Traditionally, public school boards in Manitoba perceive their mandate to be the responsibility to plan and deliver education opportunities for Kindergarten to Grade 12 students; not adults.

On the front wall of the Seine River School Division board room in Lorette is a copy of the Division's logo and beneath that a vision statement. It reads, "Leading the Way to Personal Growth." As decision time approached, one of the Trustees, Randy Engel, pointed to the vision statement, "Leading the Way to Personal Growth," on the front wall of the board room. He posed a question to his colleagues: "Do we really believe this? Where does it say we are leading the way to personal growth for only K-Grade 12 students?" There was a long pause and considerable reflection on his question. For students of the ALC's this little story ends well. The trustees voted to assume the responsibility to administer the ALC in Ste. Anne. What a great example of how vision, beliefs and values can drive decision making.

Our experiences of establishing a list of core ethical values in Seine River continued.

In November of 2004, I attended a national conference of School Superintendents in Ottawa. Dr. Avis Glaze conducted one of the sessions at this conference. Her presentation stated the case for introducing character education in Canada's public schools. I was an immediate convert to the notion.

In April of 2005, the Board of Trustees of Seine River School Division adopted the goal of developing an approach to incorporating character education into classrooms across the division. I was on a steering committee of educators tasked with developing a plan. It was during the literature review on the topic of character education that I became aware of the definition of a core ethical value. Others have used the terms, virtue, attribute, or universal principle to define a core ethical value.

When asked to list some important values, people will respond with words such as: honesty, creativity, respect, humour, curiosity, empathy, perseverance, and humility. But are these values of equal importance in guiding belief systems and actions? They are not.

To be defined as a core ethical value, it must;

1. Affirm human dignity;

2. Contribute to the welfare and development of the individual;

3. Promote the common good;

4. Be something we all have a responsibility to follow;

5. Describes a way we would want to be treated (it is reciprocal);

6. We would want everyone to act this way in similar situation (it is universal).

If we apply this definition to: honesty, respect, empathy, and humility, we find that these values pass the test as a core ethical value.

What about creativity, humour, perseverance, and curiosity? In the right circumstance and exercised in the right manner, these values can be positive. However, think about the Nazi scientists and political strategists who used curiosity and perseverance to design better genocide methods during the Second World War. These values were not used to promote the common good in that context. Therefore, I was taught that these values are best defined as supporting values, rather than core ethical values. They can be used to promote the common good, but not uniquely.

Core Ethical Values	Supporting Ethical Values
Honesty	Creativity
Respect	Humour
Empathy	Perseverance
Responsibility	Curiosity
Humility	Determined

The five core ethical values listed in the left column are universal: they are contained in all the great cultures and religions in the world. If you listed your personal core ethical values, what would they be? How would you use them to be the foundation of your character and your leadership?

Chapter Seven Key Takeaways

Great leaders believe in and use their core ethical values to guide their actions.

Make a distinction between core and supporting values.

CHAPTER 8 –
Happiness and Subjective Well-Being

"Happiness is a very small desk, and a very large wastebasket."
– Robert Orben

The leadership role can take its toll on one, especially if we continually feel stressed. When you perceive a threat, your nervous system responds by releasing a flood of stress hormones, including adrenaline and cortisol. These hormones rouse the body and prepare if for fight or flight. Your heart pounds faster, muscles tighten, blood pressure rises, breath quickens, and your senses become sharper. These physical changes increase your strength and stamina. As I mentioned earlier, this is a primitive response going back to our caveman days: eat and don't get eaten. Even though we don't really need to worry about getting eaten in the workplace (physical attack) our body reacts the same way to what we perceive to be personal, emotional attacks. Our body's emergency response system does not differentiate between a real and an imagined threat.

Living in a heightened state of hormonal arousal is not good for our health, happiness, and well-being.

What is happiness? You will recall the earlier quote by Victor Frankl who stated that neither happiness nor success can be pursued. Rather, they ensue.

Most of us probably don't believe we need a formal definition of happiness. It simply is a way of feeling about the world and our place in it. We often equate happiness with emotions such as joy, pride, and contentment. However, researchers like precise definitions. Positive psychology researcher, Sonja Lyubomirsky, describes happiness as "the experience of joy, contentment, or positive well-being combined with a sense that one's life is good, meaningful and worthwhile."

I personally connect with the thought that happiness and well-being are consistent with a life well lived; when we feel that our life has meaning, has purpose and is worthwhile. In this sense, our personal happiness and well-being is tied directly to and influenced by the type of leadership model we subscribe to.

Importance of Attitude

How we choose to view our lives and the challenges that come our way is a key determinant of our level of happiness and well being. The classic saying, "Is the glass half full or half empty?", is well entrenched in the literature of the importance of attitude. I consider myself to be a person with a positive mindset and choose to see problems as growth opportunities. When someone once asked me why I was always so positive, I replied, "I have tried the alternative (i.e. being negative) and that did not work for me."

I have a wonderful story in the vein of the glass half full/glass half empty metaphor. It has to do with one of my favourite all time golf heroes: Tom Watson. For those of you who are not professional golf fans, Tom Watson was the best golfer in the game between the reins of Jack Nicklaus and Tiger Woods. He won 39 PGA events and eight major championships. In 2009, just a few months short of his 60'th birthday, Tom had a one stroke lead playing the final hole of the British Open, one of Golf's "majors." While he ended up bogeying the last hole and then lost the tournament in a playoff, he certainly was an example to me of what we can achieve if we stay healthy, take a positive view of life and believe in the possible. Had he won that tournament, he would have been, by far, the oldest major championship winner ever. How did he play so well so long? The following simple but well known golf story holds a deep truth about the importance of attitude.

Mark Long and Nick Seitz wrote an article in the September 2012 edition of Golf Digest called "Caddie Chatter." In the article, they repeated a story told by Watson's long time caddie, Bruce Edwards. Edwards had caddied for Watson many years and then briefly for Greg Norman, another prominent golfer of that era, before returning to caddie for Watson. When asked to compare the two golfers, Edwards replied, "Let's say you are three under for the day but you drive it in a divot on hole 16. Norman would look at me and say, 'Bruce, can you believe my bad luck?' Tom would look at the ball, look at the divot and say, 'Bruce, watch this', (with every intention of pulling off a great shot).

> *Try being positive. It is better than the alternative.*

One of my favourite Watson quotes is, "If you want to increase your success rate, double your failure rate." Along with his skill, Watson had a great attitude. The divot was half full! Try being positive. It is better than the alternative.

What is your internal life story?

We all have a life story to tell. It turns out that how we run this internal narrative has a lot to do with our mental health. The way you tell your life's story matters.

In her book, *Presence: Bringing your Boldest Self to your Biggest Challenges*, Amy Cuddy, writes that four narrative themes emerge when people tell their life stories:

1. Agency – people felt they were in control of their lives;

2. Communion – people describe their lives as being about relationships;

3. Redemption – people felt that challenges had improved their attitudes or conferred wisdom in some way;

4. Contamination – people felt that positive beginnings had turned toward negative endings.

I am not sure about the wisdom part, but when I tell my life story it is a story of redemption; I see myself as having learned and grown from my humble beginnings and my crucibles.

Cuddy goes on to relate how we tell our life story has a big impact on our mental health:

"Those whose narratives fell into the three positive categories: agency, communion, and redemption, experienced significant positive mental health trajectories in the following years. But people who described their lives in terms of contamination experienced poorer mental health. And the relationship between the narratives and the health outcomes were even stronger for people who were facing significant challenges, such as major illness, divorce or losing a loved one."[10]

Personal Seven Point Happiness/Wellness Model

In addition to adopting a positive attitude, I have my own layman's seven-point happiness/wellness model that works for me. These are the type of mindsets and actions that can greatly reduce the amount of fight or flight hormones that enter and remain in your bloodstream.

You will notice from my list that most of them are about focusing on others and not being self-absorbed. If we want to find purpose and meaning in our lives, we must begin by reaching out to others.

1. **Engage in random acts of kindness.**

    Random acts of kindness have the potential to greatly enhance the well-being of both the giver and the receiver. The act does not have to be complicated.

    How many of you have been in a heavy traffic flow when two lanes suddenly converge into one? You know what happens. One of two things. Someone signals and would like to cut in. Do you get road rage and think, "Wait your turn buddy. You should have moved over a mile back." Or do you engage in a simple act of random kindness, slow down and let the other person in. I don't know if this is a Manitoba social norm, but once the person cuts in, he/she will almost always acknowledge your gesture with a wave in the rear-view mirror. Win-win. Everyone feels a little bit better about themselves and humanity in general. And your blood pressure goes down.

    I have another more personal random act of kindness example I would like to share and how it had a positive impact on me. This act took place during my two-year stint as the Principal of Ste. Anne School. I have already chronicled the stressful time that was for me.

    At the end of most school days I would leave the building and help supervise the bus loading zone. Some days that was a cold and windy assignment. On one particularly stressful day I had just returned to my office and was taking off my coat. In walked the school guidance counsellor, Rob Woods, and handed me a can of Coke.

He commented, "you look a bit frazzled, maybe this will help." He knew I liked coke soft drinks.

Years later, when Rob was in another school, I commented to him how much I had appreciated his acts of kindness when he would bring me a can of Coke at the end of a rough day. I was surprised when he asked me, "Roy, do you know how many times I brought you a Coke?" When I admitted I didn't, he responded, "It was just that one time."

Obviously, it is not the quantity but the quality of the act of random kindness that matters the most, for both the giver and the receiver. Its impact can be enduring.

2. **Concentrate on what you should be grateful for.**

Some people in the world see the glass half full and some see it half empty. Here in Manitoba we enjoy one of the highest standards of living in the world. We have food, shelter, the opportunity for meaningful work, affordable health care and a great public education system.

Why then do so many of us dwell on what we don't have, erroneously thinking that somehow having more "things" or greater social status will make us happier?

In his book, *A Whole New Mind*[11], Daniel Pink quoted some interesting information regarding the association of happiness and material wealth. In his book, he states that while the standard of living in North America has risen three-fold since 1950, there has been no appreciable increase in the levels of happiness that people are reporting. Not only can money not buy love, apparently neither does it have a big impact on our happiness. Pink goes on to profess that true happiness comes when we realize a sense of purpose in our lives.

Try taking the time each day to write down a list of five things you are grateful for. This will make you a happier person. I don't necessarily do this every day, but when I do, my whole world seems to open. We have enough "stuff." What are we grateful for? I am sure that like me, your list will have more to do with people and relationships than "stuff."

3. **Practice "CALF"**

    CALF is an anagram that represents four actions that can significantly enhance your well-being and the quality of your relationships with others:

    a **Compassion**

    By being empathetic, we can have compassion for the condition of others, rather than being judgemental. It helps us understand the reasons for people's actions. There is an old saying that, "no one gets up in the morning wanting to be an asshole." The exercise of compassion allowed me to empathize with the stress Mrs. X was going through as she tried to access transportation for her son. Being compassionate allowed me to work harder with her to resolve her situation. It helped me refrain from defensiveness, made me feel better about myself and it made me feel very, very happy.

    b **Acceptance**

    For me, acceptance has a twofold significance. When I think of being on the acceptance end of this mindset I think of my Mother. Some of my siblings have commented, "In Mom's eyes, you could do no wrong." Her unconditional acceptance was an enormous support.

The other variation on acceptance is when we can accept ourselves for who we are and accept others for who they are. This reduces stress.

c **Love/Caring**

What more can we say about love. It does make the world go around! Don't be shy in expressing it.

Dennis and Roy 1991

One of my best friends was a man named Dennis Thompson. For more than 25 years we golfed together, played ball together and often had various forms of refreshment while reflecting on our golf scores and on life in general. In 2000, Denis was diagnosed with stomach cancer and subsequently had his stomach removed. He recovered from that and was even able to take up golfing again. Sadly, about a year after the surgery, the cancer returned and I was made aware of the term, "secondary reoccurrence." When cancer returns a second time, it is almost always fatal within a short period.

By August of 2002, Dennis had been sent home from the hospital and was receiving palliative care. I would visit him often, and on one occasion, he asked me if I would give the eulogy at his funeral. Pause. Deep breath. Although I was very anxious about the request, of course, I agreed. I began working on his eulogy; unnerving when the person is still alive.

By mid October, I was visiting Dennis and we were watching a World Series baseball game together. Without warning, he blurted out, "Roy, how is my eulogy coming?" I told him I was almost done. What he asked next should not have surprised me, but it did catch me off guard. He said, "Could I hear it now?" I promised to bring it with me on my next visit.

In Dennis' eulogy, I used the analogy of life being like a game of golf. There were many parallels between Dennis' approach to life and his approach to golf. Golf reflects the cycle of life itself. No matter what you shoot, the next time you play, you have to go back to the first tee and begin all over again and try and do better than the day before. Dennis did that in his life. When he contracted cancer, he did not lie down and quit. Even in very weak condition, we played a round of golf in Winkler on August 8, a little over two months before he passed away.

I wrote how he was so courageous. In golf Dennis hated to take the safe shot: he believed in the adage, "no risk, no reward." He lived his life that way. In his last days, he dealt with several issues regarding arrangements for his own funeral. This was not a guy that was in avoidance.

So, a week before he passed away on October 22, 2002, I paid Dennis one of my last visits. I read Dennis the eulogy I had prepared. First, we cried. Then we laughed. Dennis said to me, "Roy, you bastard. Why didn't you tell me all these nice things before now?" Yes indeed. Why had I not?

They say that on our own deathbed, it will not be the things in life that we did that we will regret. It will be the things we wish we had done, but did not. So, if you have someone who you care for, don't wait for them to ask you to write their eulogy to express your love and caring. By then it is too late and you won't be able to take full advantage of the curative powers of expressing love.

d **Forgiveness**

Of the four mindsets, this is the one that is the hardest to act out. For most of my youth and young adulthood I harboured some very negative emotions towards my father and the circumstances he placed us in. These were destructive feelings that only contributed to a tendency to engage in acts of self-pity and anger. Neither emotion was contributing to my happiness and well-being.

When truth be told, my Dad had a lot of positive qualities. He was a true bon vivant and admired by many. He was a fine baseball player and a crack shot when hunting. He was very good at tinkering with all things mechanical. He had many friends and hence his nickname, Bud. He was everyone's buddy. He was also very creative. I remember a story that demonstrates this quality.

My Dad and a friend of his, Joe Martel, had cut a large load of cedar and jack pine fence posts, hoping to sell them to a local lumberyard. When they arrived at the lumberyard, the owner bought the cider posts but refused to buy the lower quality jack pine posts. They left Joe's phone number as a contact. Dad and Joe went home. The next day, Joe had someone call the lumber yard and ask if they had any jack pine fence posts for sale? Ten minutes later, a lumber yard employee called to say they wanted to buy the fence posts. I recall stories of Dad and Joe having a hearty laugh each time they drove by the lumber yard. The posts sat there, untouched for years.

Years later, when I became more aware of the hardships he had endured as a young man, I could replace judgement with compassion and forgive. It was a big and unnecessary load off my shoulders. Try letting go. It is very therapeutic.

Backyard view from the deck in Giroux

4. **Take time for solitude and reflection**

   I enjoy golfing. No, I love golfing. It is not just the game itself I love, but I love the time spent outdoors in nature. No phones. No email.

   We all need to find quiet time to just sit and reflect. Slow things down and complicated issues start to sort themselves out. One of my unstructured reflections times takes place on the deck at the back of our house in Giroux. Sometimes I sit and think. Sometimes I just sit; watch the humming birds, admire my lawn.

5. **Maintain healthy relationships**

   A major stressor for many people is the unsatisfactory inter-personal relationships at work, at home and in the community. I love Stephen Covey's metaphor of the emotional bank account. He claimed that we must build an emotional bank account with our acquaintances just as we build a financial bank account. You need to continue to make deposits for your account to grow. We make deposits in emotional bank accounts with others by acting with integrity. By keeping our promises and by not speaking about people behind their backs.

   Like a financial bank account, an emotional bank account can withstand the occasional withdrawal if it is in a strong enough net position.

6. **Physical "stuff"**

   a   Eat properly

   When I was younger and had a lot more energy than I do now, I used to joke that eating and sleeping were heavily overrated. That was an example of childish bravado that I would come to regret. I would often go to work and subsist on nothing but coffee, sometimes even skipping lunch. Not good. Now if I am in a rush, I will at least have a protein shake and glass of orange juice before going out the door. Fuel the body, fuel the mind.

b   Exercise

I would wager that most people reading this know that it is important for our health and effective functioning that we exercise moderately at least three times a week for thirty minutes. But remember we said that people will do something they feel to be safe, possible and valuable. Most of us could spend thirty minutes taking a brisk walk three times a week. It would be safe and possible. So why aren't we doing it? Because we are not convinced of the value and don't have the desire to do it. Even with my increased access to discretionary time in my current work schedule, I still must strive to work out three times a week.

c   Get enough sleep

Donald Trump once pontificated that, "If you want to be a billionaire, sleep as little as possible." Like many of his other pronouncements on his run to the American Presidency, this one is very suspect if not downright false. In their book, *Sleeping Your Way to the Top*, Cralle, Brown, and Cane assert, "Sleep is a fundamental need that can't be short changed without incurring serious negative consequences. Whether in the workplace, at home, or in school, if you wish to be a success, sleep needs to be your friend, not your foe."[12]

Data shared in this book states there are three type of people when it comes to the amount of sleep we need:

    a   "Short Sleepers" – people who can get by with 5 hours of sleep a night. This group makes up only 3-5% of the population

    b   "Long Sleepers" – people who need 10 – 12 hours of sleep a night and make up to 3 – 5% of the population

    c   "Normal Sleepers" – the 90% of the population that requires 7 – 9 hours of sleep per night.

I personally am a "long sleeper." If you are a long sleeper, and can get over the perception of being lazy, make sure you get your nine hours sleep each night!

I have one more recommendation for you regarding sleep. Take a nap at lunch time. If you are able, close your door, darken the room, put your feet up and nod off! The recuperative power of a ten-minute nap has been scientifically proven. Try it. You will be amazed how refreshed and alert you will be for the afternoon. I know it worked for me.

7. **MOST IMPORTANT: Find your flow: what is your purpose, your life's higher meaning?**

I have saved the most important determinant of happiness and well-being for the last point. The purpose of life is a life of purpose. We find purpose in things both large and small: in our personal lives and in our work. When we are clear about that purpose and act on it regularly, I guarantee you will be a happier and a healthier person.

Men and women in Okinawa, Japan, live on average seven years longer than North Americans and have the longest disability-free life expectancy on Earth. The little island of Okinawa has been called the land of the immortals. There are more people over a hundred years old there than anywhere.

Researchers from National Geographic studied the people living on Okinawa to see if they could find what the determinates were that accounted for the longevity of the people living there. There were some obvious things such as eating habits: they ate off smaller plates and stopped eating when they were 80% full (Not sure how they measured that!).

Something else more significant emerged. Unlike their western counterparts, they don't retire! They don't even have a word that translates into "retirement." They don't recognize the concept of stopping work completely. However, they do have a related word which is *ikigai*. The rough translation of this word is, "the reason to wake up in the morning." It is their purpose for living.

In the western world, prosperity and the standard of living has more than tripled since 1950, and earlier retirements became more accessible and popular (remember "freedom fifty-five?"). As Daniel Pink pointed out, during the same period, 1950 – 2000, numerous surveys of peoples' levels of happiness and contentment revealed that this measure stated the same. More affluence did not translate into happier people.

As we get older, we should not think of retirement as a time when we shut it down. That is not healthy. We should be thinking of how we can transition in our lives in a way that we can continue to seek purpose and meaning and to continue to contribute to making the world a better place. You will live longer. You will be happier and more effective in whatever you undertake. Just ask the ninety-six-year-old Okinawan who defeated a former boxing champion in his thirties.

Don't retire in the sense that you shut everything down. And if possible resist the urge to enter or be placed in an old folks' home. These places can be depressing. Unless there is some intervention, residents have no reason for getting up in the morning. It doesn't have to be that way. Healthy aging in a nursing home can happen, but people who live there need to see that there lives continue to have purpose and meaning. In the 1970's, Ellen Langer and Judith Rodin conducted a heart rending psychology experiment with residents of a nursing home.

They selected a group of seniors and gave each of them a house plant for their rooms. Half the seniors were told not to touch the plant; the nurses would take care of it for them. The other half were told that it would become their responsibility to care for plant, to keep it alive and flourishing. After half a year, the psychologists followed up with the two groups. Those who were given the responsibility to care for their plant tested to be more alert, cheerful, active and healthy. They also lived longer. It is a comment both sad and yet inspiring that given a purpose as simple as looking after a plant can have such a positive impact on our happiness and well-being.

Be clear about what you want to do with your life. Remember, you will not write your own eulogy or define your own legacy. You only leave behind the raw material that was your life for others to assess, summarize and eulogize.

In many of the workshops I conduct, I facilitate an exercise, inspired by Stephen Covey, that gets the participants to think about who they want to be and what they want to do in life. I ask them to visualize sitting in the balcony of a church looking down at the proceedings at a funeral. There is a body lying in an open casket. Two people get up and each deliver a eulogy about the deceased. The speakers are a family member of the deceased and someone from the person's work life. As they begin, you realize that you are the person in the coffin. What will they say about you? What would you want them to say? Remember, you do not write your own legacy or your own eulogy. You only leave behind the raw material and the memories of your life from which someone else will write the eulogy. Now is the time to start building those memories you would like to have recalled.

People have often shared with me that there is a disconnect between how they see their lives unfolding and how they would want to be remembered. No one on his or her death bed ever said, "Gee…I wish I would have spent more time at work and earned more money." If you are feeling that disconnect, why wait for your funeral? That will be too late. Why not start acting now like the person who you want described in your eulogy and achieving your true purpose in life?

Key Takeaways from Chapter 8

- Our "internal narrative," how we perceive our life to have unfolded, is a major factor in our attitude and consequently in our mental health. We can learn to change our narrative to be more positive.

- We are happier and healthier when we focus less on ourselves and more on the well-being of others: happiness ensues!

- The most important determinant of good health and longevity is to see the meaning and purpose of your life.

- Adopt a "death bed" mentality; and don't sweat the small stuff!

PART THREE – LESSONS IN
Leadership –
Interpersonal Skills

INTRODUCTION TO PART THREE

When it comes to identifying successful leaders, I am biased by my reading and my own beliefs and experiences to emphasize the importance of the inner strength and character of the leader as being paramount. However, as my career advanced I soon realized that just being a nice fellow alone would not cut it. A level of expertise and competence is also necessary.

I used to avail myself of the services of a local mechanic. Nice fellow. I really liked him. He told good stories and laughed a lot. He also needed to make a living, so for years I supported him. He had no formal mechanical training, and in the late 60's prior to the introduction of computers in cars, he could provide a reasonably good oil change and tune up. But he did not stay current. It got to the point where he would fix something on my car, but two more problems would crop up because of his tinkering. Nice fellow with no competence and expertise. We had to part ways.

Leadership is like that. We must keep learning to stay current. We must develop our expertise and competence. In Part Three I will share some of the leadership skills and processes that I have learned, sometimes the hard way, over the years.

CHAPTER 9 –
Employee Supervision – Evaluation, and Discipline

In the last chapter I made the point that leaders use their beliefs and core ethical values to drive their actions. Nowhere is this more important than the leader's beliefs and values regarding employee evaluation and discipline.

Why do we "evaluate" employees anyway?

In 2000 in Seine River School Division we took on the task of firming up our employee supervision and evaluation practices. I took the leadership role of meeting with employee groups to get them involved in this process. The first group I addressed was the school custodian group. I had a presentation prepared but decided use the discovery approach from my teaching days to ask the custodians, "Why do we evaluate employees?" One of our senior custodians sitting in the front row raised his hand and answered, "That is something that happens before you get fired." Clearly, we had some work to do.

Ironically, the custodian was referencing one of the answers I was looking for. Like it or not there are two basic reasons why we conduct formal evaluations of employees:

Why?

1. **Accountability** - Are they doing the job they were hired do?

2. **Growth** – Through the process of evaluation can we identify areas of growth for the employee?

There are two more factors that I believe form the 4 "Pillars" of employee evaluation. The other two answer to the question of, "how?"

How?

3. **Regular** – A clear evaluation schedule needs to be adopted, communicated, and adhered to; no surprises and don't use the employee evaluation just to fire people.
4. **Planned** – The evaluation process needs to be defined including criteria to be used and timelines.

The Four Pillars of Employee Evaluation

Why	How
Accountability	**Regular**
New employees	Regular scheculed, not ad-hoc
New assignments	
Encountering difficulty	
Growth	**Planned**
Learn new skills	PGM or Clinical
Improve existing skills	Criteria

An externally imposed evaluation is more suitable for new employees, employees in new assignments or employees clearly encountering difficulties: are they doing the job they were hired to do?

I have no problem with being honest about the reasons we evaluate employees. The problem I have is how we institutionalize practices to achieve those stated goals. For instance, do we need to evaluate every employee every year for the purposes of accountability? No. What a waste of time and other resources.

In his book, *Get Rid of the Performance Review*, Samuel Culbert states: "It's time to put the performance review out of its misery. This corporate sham is one of the most insidious, most damaging, and yet most ubiquitous of corporate activities. Everybody does it, and almost everyone who's evaluated hates it. It's a pretentious, bogus practice that produces absolutely nothing that any thinking executive should call a corporate plus."[13]

Strong words. I don't know if I would get rid of the performance review (evaluation) completely, but I am in total agreement that this process is heavily overused, sometimes with very negative results.

Several years ago, I had the pleasure of attending a workshop conducted by Dr. Pasi Salsberg, renowned Finnish educator and scholar. He was brought to Manitoba to speak to educators about the conditions in his country that were contributing to very successful learning outcomes for all students. There were several contributing factors. One I found very interesting was the esteem in which teachers were held as professionals in Finland. They were treated and compensated on par with other professionals such as doctors and lawyers. When asked about how teachers were evaluated in Finland he responded: "We do not speak of this. It is irrelevant in our country. Instead we discuss how can we help them." Clearly a different approach than the traditional clinical supervision model.

In SRSD we found that only 1-3% of teachers required an externally directed performance review approach. Given our teacher count of approximately two hundred teachers that meant that only 2-6 teachers a year required that type of supervisory experience. Another 17 – 19, either new teachers or teachers in new assignments, could benefit from some external performance feedback and direct coaching.

That meant that approximately 80% of our teaching staff was working at or well above the minimum competency required as a classroom teacher. Yet, at one time all teachers received the externally driven performance review every three years. Those teachers did not need a judgemental and directive process to tell them what they needed to do to keep growing. Ultimately, we introduced a Personal Growth Model that put the teacher in charge of his/her own growth. Under this model, it was the teachers that decided what they would like to work on, how they would like to work on it and with whom they would work. It was a model predicated on growth not accountability.

There are some leaders whose belief system says something like, left alone people will not grow. I do not believe that. I know that was not true for me and since I am nothing special, I know it is not true for most teachers. I did not find external performance reviews motivational in the least. I understood that it was about accountability and I could live with that. But the motivation for true growth comes from within, not an external demand.

Teacher Supervisory Continuum

Percentage of Teacher Population	Supervisor Interventions		
80%	Listening	Provide for ongoing growth	Non-Directive
	Clarifying		PGM
	Encouraging		
17-19%	Presenting	Some need for improvement	Collaborative
	Interacting		PGM/Clinical
	Counteracting		
1-3%	Modeling	"NEAT"	Directive
	Directing	Needs Improvement	Clinical
	Judging	Explain what must happen	
		Assistance will be given	
		Time that will be given	

What about that 1-3%? As in any other occupation is it possible that not all people are cut out to be teachers? Of course, the answer is yes. However, in all fairness we need to be clear with those individuals and give them the opportunity to improve. After all, they did spend 4 to 5 years getting their teaching degrees.

A fair process to assess any occupation does not have to be complex; only honest and clear. We used a process referred to by the acronym, NEAT: needs improvement, explain what must happen, assistance will be given, and the amount of time that will be given to make the required improvement.

It takes a skilled supervisor to conduct a performance review of a struggling employee. Let's be honest. No one likes having their faults and weaknesses identified and recorded. Even the non-struggling employee tends to get defensive when someone identifies a weakness. That's what we have spouses for!

If the result of a performance review is going to lead to a recommendation for dismissal, the best that can happen is that even if the employee does not agree, they will grant that it was a fair process and they believed in the honesty and competency of the person who conducted the review. Easy to say; hard to do.

Employee Motivation

When I was entering the supervisor/manager ranks back in the 1970's it was a fairly common belief that employee behaviour could be shaped by positive and negative reinforcement theory. Reward the good behaviour and punish the bad behaviour. The theory went that this would result in more positive behaviour and extinguish the bad behaviour. We employed this approach with our children so why wouldn't it be an acceptable approach in the workplace? Wrong. It proves to be wrong both at home and in the workplace. Once again, we see the thinking that some sort of external intervention is needed to get the right responses out of people.

Intuitively, I have always known that true motivation for good behaviour and personal growth is an internal condition. As leaders, we need to be very cautious when we start to think that, "I know the secret to motivating people." I am always leery with people who think they are that charismatic and powerful, because I don't believe anyone truly has that power. The best we can do, I believe, is inspire, by way of a good example, others to be more inclined to be self-motivated. In the end, people motivate themselves, but leaders can provide a leadership style that encourages and enables employees to motivate themselves. How? I will give you a hint. It is not with performance reviews! You can lead a horse to water but you can't make it drink; unless you salt the oats.

As I mentioned earlier, I have been greatly influenced by the work of Daniel Pink and the books he has written. In his most recent book, *Drive: The Surprising Truth About What Motivates Us*, he states that, "Carrots and sticks are so last century. For 21'st century work, we need to upgrade to autonomy, mastery, and purpose."[14]

Leaders who provide employees with these three factors will find they have a very self-motivated and engaged work force.

Leaders provide for employee ***autonomy*** when, as much as possible, they allow the employee the latitude to work on what they want to work on, when they want to work on it, how they want to work on it and with whom they want to work. The level of autonomy depends on the type of work to be accomplished as well as other constraints such as timelines.

Leaders provide for employee ***mastery*** by providing the encouragement and resources for the employee to improve: professional development resources, time away from work to attend workshops, allowing time to mentor and be mentored by others are some examples. As I mentioned, I was provided with this type of support as CEO in SRSD; I was very self-motivated as a result. It is also important for the leader to model the mindset of continuous improvement.

Employees who believe that there is a higher ***purpose*** to their work are the most self-motivated of all. Leaders can be a role model in this regard. They need to lead the charge in public statements about the importance of the work they do and help employees do the same.

I am the co-owner of my own business. I have almost complete control of what I work on, when and how I work on it and whom I might choose to work with me. I have the time and resources to continue to read, learn and grow. And finally, I work to support people in the public education system. What a great purpose. I have the best job in the world!

Employee Discipline - Culpable and Non-Culpable Behaviour

One of the most stressful but important responsibilities of a leader is dealing with unacceptable behaviour in the workplace. The material that follows is a conglomerate of ideas and materials that I gathered during my leadership career that assisted me in making sound decisions regarding employee misbehaviour. You will recall that one of my first employee discipline issues I dealt with as a new Superintendent in 1995 that did not end up well. I wish I had relied more on the following information back then. I would have ended up making a better decision.

The first step is to determine if the unacceptable behaviours are culpable or non-culpable.

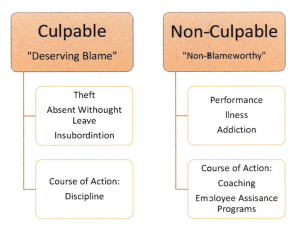

Competency Issues:

Non-culpable behaviour often involves issues of competency. The employee is not fully responsible or deserving of blame. The supervisory approach should be one that provides for skill building; a non-disciplinary approach.

Resources should be provided to help the employee meet the required level of competence. Failure to meet the minimum standard may result in further action including discharge.

Conduct Issues:

Culpable behaviour requires progressive discipline, unless the incident results in a fundamental breach of the employee-employer relationship, such as theft or the assault of another. In cases such as these, some form of immediate action, such as termination, may be the only recourse.

The employee knows what is required and can do what is required but chooses to act in a way contrary to requirements.

A **discipline** approach focuses on what the employee must learn to bring his/her behaviour in line with the needs and expectations of the organization. Consequences such as progressive discipline will come to bear if the required change is not made. **Punishment**, however, tends to apply negative sanctions, expecting that those negative sanctions will have some sort of deterrent effect. Punishment tends to drive the undesirable behaviour underground, not cure it.

Establishing Cause for Discipline (Culpable Behaviour)

Before determining the appropriate consequences for unacceptable behaviour, the leader must determine if he/she is dealing with culpable behaviour. Ask these questions:

1. Was the employee given warning of the possible or probable disciplinary consequence of his/her conduct? ("Ought to have known")

2. Was the rule or order reasonably related to the efficient and safe operation of his/her professional responsibility?

3. Did the employer try to discover whether the employee did, in fact, violate a rule or order of the management?

4. Was the employer's investigation conducted fairly and objectively?

5. Did the investigation produce substantial evidence of proof that the employee was culpable (guilty as alleged)?

6. Had the employer applied its rules, orders, and penalties without discrimination?

If the answer to any of these questions is yes, we probably have culpable behaviour subject to discipline.

Assessing the Appropriate Disciplinary Penalty

Once the behaviour is considered to be culpable, take into consideration the following mitigating factors before determining the appropriate discipline.

1. **The seriousness of the misconduct**

    The more serious the infraction, the less room there is for discretion in assessing the disciplinary measures.

2. **Seniority**

    Length of service can impact on the discipline. Is this a new employee or someone who has been with the organization for a significant period?

3. **Disciplinary record**

    Is this a first time or a repeat offender?

4. **Correction, rehabilitation, and deterrence**

    Will the penalty result in changed behaviour?

5. **Provocation**

    Was he/she provoked?

6. **Employee's state of mind**

    Are there extenuating circumstances in the person's life? Were his/her actions planned and continued over time?

7. **Admission of guilt**

Has he/she admitted and expressed genuine regret, indicating this would never happen again?

8. **Personal circumstances**

   What will be the economic impact on this employee and his/her family if he/she is terminated?

9. **Consistency of discipline**

   Have other employees in similar situations been given the same or similar penalties?

10. **Condonation**

    Has his/her misconduct been condoned in the past?

Progressive Discipline

Progressive discipline means you move through increasingly stronger counselling or training in an attempt at assisting the employee to bring his or her behaviour to an acceptable level. Depending on the severity of the culpable behaviour, you need to decide where to begin on the progressive discipline scale. Steps may be skipped. Use progressive discipline for like or similar offences.

1. **Issue an Oral Warning**

- Set the time and place to ensure privacy.

- Since the meeting will be disciplinary in nature, if unionized, advise the employee he/she is entitled to bring a union representative to sit in on the meeting.

- Before the meeting, make notes about what needs to be said.

- Clearly state that you are issuing an oral warning about the unacceptable behaviour. Be specific in describing the behaviour. Give concrete examples that depict the problem you want the employee to address.

- Remind the employee of acceptable behaviour, the organization's rules and the corrective action expected and by when.

- Offer assistance as deemed appropriate.

- State the consequences of non-compliance.

- Document the meeting, placing a copy in the employees file and giving the employee a copy. If the problem persists, investigate to determine if further discipline is appropriate and at what level.

2. **Issue a Written Warning**

- Clearly state that you are issuing a written warning. Cite any existing personnel policy that supports this procedure.

- Describe in detail the behaviour problem. Give examples stated during the oral warning along with examples that occurred since that meeting. The employee needs to understand that you see no progress or insufficient progress since the oral warning was given.

- Outline previous steps taken to correct the behaviour.

- Describe the impact of the problem. Be specific. Give examples of how the employee's behaviour directly impacts the organization.

- Note the employee's explanation for the behaviour.

- Reiterate the organization's expectations. Note that if sustained improvement is not demonstrated by a specific time, further disciplinary action will be taken up to and including termination.

- Provide the letter to the employee and place a copy of the letter in his/her personnel file.

3. **Impose a Suspension**

- Normally requires the authorization of the CEO or designate at the organization.

- The suspension letter should include the details of the suspension,

- With or without pay for a specific time with the reinstatement date indicated,

- Or indefinitely pending an investigation. **Move to Terminate**

- Terminate or dismiss the employee when adequate changes to behaviours are not met within a reasonable period as required by law.

- Termination is a last resort and used only when severe, documented, non-compliance issues arise.

- Follow organizational standards, provincial law, and collective agreement.

Giving Clear Directives

A clear directive does not leave room for an employee's own interpretation. In dealing with culpable behaviour, either because we want to be a nice person or we lack the resolve, we don't always give clear enough direction. I have often dealt with employee misbehaviour, according to a supervisor. When confronted with the accusation, an employee will often claim this is the first they have heard that there was a problem. One such employee shared with me that he thought his supervisor was very happy with his work and that his last performance evaluation was positive; it was. Yet, the supervisor wanted the individual fired. The employee had not been getting a clear message regarding expectations.

	Directive	Clear	Not Clear
1.	Would you mind responding by…		X
2.	Provide your response by noon on Friday…	X	
3.	I insist that…	X	
4.	Perhaps you should…		X
5.	You are directed to…	X	
6.	You may wish to consider….		X
7.	I encourage you to come in on time….		X
8.	Any further incidents of tardiness will result in…	X	
9.	Why don't you….		X
10.	You will….	X	

Chapter 9 Key Takeaways

- We "evaluate" others for accountability and growth.

- The true motivation for good behaviour and personal growth comes from an internal drive.

- The conditions of autonomy, mastery and purpose in the workplace are the pre-requisites for self-motivation.

- Unsatisfactory employee behaviour can be culpable or non-culpable.

- When dealing with culpable behaviour, use a progressive discipline approach.

- Give clear directives.

CHAPTER 10 –
Decision Making

"All work is sacred and all work is soul work. If certain essential elements are missing from our work, such as information or the opportunity to contribute to the decisions that affect the organization and therefore our own life and livelihood, our work will deprive our souls."

– Lance Secretan

There are two implications of the above quote. As individuals, we want to have the information and that ability to be involved in organizational decision making. Additionally, as leaders, we need to ensure that the people we supervise have those same opportunities to be involved and contribute to a vibrant, positive organizational culture.

I have learned to use a simple framework to guide decision making.

The Three "C's" of Decision Making

1. **Command**

    In this mode, the leader simply makes the decision and informs others. Leaders often make these types of decisions that require low expertise and have low relevance for others. At others times a leader will make command decisions in higher stakes situations with a moral imperative at stake. Use this mode with caution.

2. **Consultative**

   In this mode, a decision is made by the leader or leadership team after consulting with others who have expertise that contributes to a good decision. The leader still reserves the right to make the final call. Be careful using this approach. You need to be clear that you are consulting, gathering information to help you make the final call. If you are not clear, others may infer that their opinion is the one that will win the day. Once the decision is taken by the leader, he/she needs to get back to those consulted in some way to explain why the decision was taken and unfolded the way it did, especially if the decision is going to be contrary to the input provided.

3. **Consensus**

   In this mode, a decision is made with full participation or with representative members of the decision-making group. Normally those involved have the expertise to participate and the decision has high relevancy for them (affects them directly in some way).

   A lesser variation of consensus group decision making is the "**majority vote**." There are advantages and disadvantages to both approaches. Majority vote is quick and dirty and creates winners and losers. Consensus ends up with a greater commitment to the final decision by participants, but the process can be long and frustrating.

Who Should You Consult?

People normally would be consulted if they have **expertise** related to the decision at hand and/or if the decision has **relevancy** for them.

Decision Making Matrix – Relevancy and Expertise

When do we consult, command or seek consensus? We need to keep in mind the concepts of expertise and relevance. I have found the matrix below useful in considering which decision making style to employ in any given situation.

If I am making a decision that has little or no impact on the people I work with and those same people have no expertise relevant to the decision in question, I would just use the command mode, make the call. If I needed to make a decision that affected no one I work with, but I know some of those people have some expertise to offer that would help in making the decision, I would consult them. If I had to make a decision that affected the people I work with but they had little or no expertise regarding the decision, I would consult. Remember it is important to get back to these people after the decision is taken to explain why it was taken, especially if the final decision went contrary to the input that was given. Quadrant #2 is where you need to employ a consensus approach: a decision that affects everyone and where those affected have a high level of expertise to offer in coming to the final decision.

Decision making is one of the key managerial areas in which the leader must make sure that he/she has their ego in check. A leader must be able to be open to being influenced to changing his/her mind when someone else has a different or better option to consider.

Another time when the leader must be humble is when he/she decides how much delegation and allowance for discretion that is allowed to those being led.

Five Levels of Initiative and Delegation

As a leader, how much initiative do you allow for people under your supervision to make decisions?

1. The employee must wait for you to tell them what to do.

2. The employee can ask what to do.

3. The employee can recommend what should be done.

4. The employee can act/decide and let you know right away.

5. The employee can act/decide and inform you later.

Discretionary Decision Making

Webster's dictionary defines discretion as the freedom to make decisions. It implies choice as opposed to a decision guided by rules, policies, or law. Interpretation and choice of rules often involve discretion. Conversely, the exercise of discretion, in many instances is guided by rules and values.

Discretion is abused when one treats unequally individuals who are relatively the same or treats equally individuals who are relatively different or unequal.

There are Two Basic Principles to Consider When Exercising Discretion

1. The Fairness Test: if the exercise of discretion is related to the personality of the offender, his/her political views, his/her race or religion, or economic status it fails the fairness test and thus is an abuse of discretion.

2. The more serious the offence the less leeway for judgement. A judge has less discretion in sentencing a convicted murderer than someone who received a speeding ticket while taking his wife to the hospital.

There can be both advantages and disadvantages of discretionary decision making.

Advantages of Discretion

1. It enables the decision-maker to consider the nuances of specific situations.

2. It allows for individualization.

3. It provides latitude to address complex decision-making situations.

4. It recognizes the education, training, expertise and experience of the decision maker.

Disadvantages of Discretion

1. It allows for disparity in decision-making.

2. It increases the opportunity for discrimination, unfairness, and injustice.

3. It leads to uncertainty.

4. It contributes to secrecy.

5. It allows for the abuse of power.

I have developed a matrix that captures the interconnection of discretion, expertise and initiative and how that relates to employee engagement. If you have an employee that has low expertise and operates at a level one of initiative, not allowing this person a lot of discretion is probably a good thing. You may ask yourself how this person got hired in the first place.

If you allow someone with low expertise and low initiative to have high discretionary decision latitude, I call this the "trouble waiting to happen" quadrant. If you have a highly skilled and expert employee who is allowed little or no discretion and who is permitted to operate at only levels 1-3 of initiative, you are going to have an employee who is bored and who is looking for somewhere else to work.

Once again, the top right quadrant, Quadrant #2, is where we want to be. This is where highly skilled employees who can operate at level 5 initiative and who are given a high degree of discretionary decision making authority. This is where the steward delegation occurs.

I came to realize later that as an Assistant Superintendent, my supervisor, the Superintendent, Mr. Suszko allowed me to work under the conditions highlighted in that top right quadrant. The autonomy and the confidence I was afforded were highly motivational.

Expertise/Initiative/Discretion Matrix

Low Expertise/High Discretion
"Waiting for trouble to happen!"

High Expertise/High Discretion
"Where you want to be."
Allows for level 5 initiative.

Low Expertise/Low Discretion
"Probably a good thing."
Level 1 Initiative

High Expertise/Low Discretion
"Boredom – people move on."
Level 1-3 Initiative only

Problems and Dilemmas – How to Frame a Situation

It is important to frame a decision-making situation as being either a problem or a dilemma. As a leader, you will be facing more dilemmas than problems. Problems are easy to solve; because of their inter-personal nature, dilemmas are not. Should we buy a new photocopier for our office? Let's do a study and check our budget. Done. Two employees are in conflict; each blaming the other for the problem and one approaches you for help. What do you do? You have a dilemma. Don't try to solve a dilemma like a problem.

Problem	Dilemma (AKA Wicked Problem)
• One right answer	• Not "answerable"
• Calls for analysis	• Calls for synthesis
• Easily recognizable and often does not involve people	• Situation is complex and usually involves more than one person
• Terminal (when it is done, you don't think about it any more)	• Do what you can to make the situation better
• You solve a problem	• You live a dilemma

You can rush to solve a problem: one answer, one right solution; simple. Unfortunately dealing with situations involving inter-personal conflict are not that easily solved and often there is no one right answer.

Final Word on Decision Making: Equality and Equity

> *I am very much opposed to the "zero tolerance" mentality.*

Leaders make hundreds of decisions every week. Some of them trivial; some of them having the potential to dramatically alter the life of an employee or an organizational goal. Appreciating the need to treat people equitably and not just equally is a key to high quality decision making.

I am very much opposed to the "zero tolerance" mentality that is found in various work places and implies everyone will be treated the same or equally, no exceptions. There is nothing so unequal as the equal treatment of unequals. In stark contrast to the zero-tolerance policy is the famous Nordstrom retail chain store one page employee handbook. It contained only one rule: "Use good judgement in all situations. There will be no additional rules." This is a company that has employees operating in the top right quadrant of discretion and initiative. It is also a company renowned for the high quality of its customer service.

If we have competent leaders and employees who conduct themselves with a high degree of integrity, give them the latitude for discretion in decision making. In the end, everyone benefits.

Chapter 10 Key Takeaways

- Consider the appropriate use of the three "C's" of decision making: command, consult, consensus.

- Consider expertise and relevance when involving others in decision making.

- Allow employees the latitude for discretion in decision making.

- You solve a problem; you live a dilemma.

- Be prepared to consider equity as well as equality in decision making.

CHAPTER 11 –
Dealing with Change

"The only people who want a change are babies with a dirty diaper."
– Jean Suszko

Do you remember where you were and what was on your mind New Year's Eve 1999? You might not remember where you were, but I would be willing to wager that you or some one else brought up the topic of Y2K.

Many people were predicting catastrophe when the clock hit midnight and ushered in the year 2000. Fears of disaster were being fuelled by an assumption made when computers were first being programmed.

In the minds of some people, this problem was the result of the fact that most dates in computers automatically assumed that the date, at that time, began with "19" as in 1990. So, when the date was to turn from December 31, 1999 to January 1, 2000, it was prophesied by some that the computers would malfunction and shut down. Since almost every aspect of everyday life was being run by computers including, banks, traffic lights, airplanes, and micro wave ovens, it was feared that the Y2K bug was going to bring an end to civilization. Conspiracy theorists were having a field day.

Well, we are still here and as the new year came in the Y2K scare was soon forgotten.

What was not forgotten, and what was underscored by the Y2K scare was the importance that technology was assuming in society. This was the case in education. Starting in the mid 80's and early 90's those of us in education realized that technology was going to play an increasingly important role not only as an administrative tool but also as a support to classroom instruction. Discussions with school principals began leading into the new century and post Y2K regarding technology literacy. Everyone agreed that our principals and teachers needed to become more technologically literate. The speed of change being ushered in regarding the use of technology was accelerating. But how would we do that? How would we adapt to the changing technological landscape?

Framework for Change

By the year 2005 I had done a lot of professional development work around change theory. After 10 years as a CEO I also had a lot of practical experience in dealing with accepting change and helping others do the same. I have come to believe that people will support and attempt something new if they feel it is safe, possible, and most importantly valuable to do.

Top Ten Reasons Why Proposed Changes Failed

I am also aware of ten reasons why changes fail. They are all subsets of the three circles in the Venn diagram above.

1. People leading the change think that announcing the change is the same as implementing it. (Knowledge)

2. People's concerns with change are not surfaced or addressed. (Desire)

3. Those being asked to change are not involved in planning the change. (Knowledge)

4. No compelling reason has been put forward for the change. (Desire/Value)

5. The change leadership team doesn't include early adopters, resistors, and informal leaders. (Knowledge)

6. The change isn't piloted so the organization doesn't learn what's needed to support the change. (Ability)

7. Leaders lose focus and/or fail to prioritize, causing "death by 1000 initiatives." (Value/Desire)

8. People are not enabled or encouraged to build new skills. (Ability)

9. Those leading the change aren't credible: they under-communicate, give mixed messages, and do not model the behaviours the change requires. (Desire/Knowledge/Ability)

10. Progress is not measured; how do we know the change made a difference? (Value/Desire)

What this tells me is that if you have a good idea, but no implementation plan, your odds of getting the desired change are not good.

What's Responsible for Change Failures: Value of the Idea or Implementation?

	Bad Idea Good implementation 10%	Good Idea Good Implementation 10%
Quality of Implementation	Bad Idea Bad Implementation 10%	Good Idea Bad Implementation 70%

Value of the idea
Source: David Nadler, *Navigating Change*

David Nadler claimed that a good implementation plan supports a good idea only 10% of the time. Surely, we can do better than that. A bad implementation plan supports a good idea 70% of the time, thus dooming the good idea to failure.

How did we use this knowledge regarding change to help our staff become more technologically literate? Simply coming up with an idea at central office and announcing it was not a sound way to approach change. Remember the concepts of relevance and expertise? While the principals and teachers may not have had the expertise at that time to design a program for increasing technological literacy, any such plan would be of the utmost relevancy to them. They needed to be involved in the design and implementation of the plan.

We had regular discussions with the Principals. They agreed that we needed to be more deliberate about increasing the knowledge of how to best use technology, especially to help improve student learning. Initially they were proposing that the answer to increase technological expertise at the school level was to hire a staff member in each school that would be the technology expert. We moved away from this approach, feeling that the required depth and breadth of knowledge would stop with one individual, the expert.

> *You can't learn to play a musical instrument by reading about the history of music. You must play the instrument.*

We gravitated towards a model in which every principal and teacher would be given a desk top computer for their personal use in every classroom and office. You can't learn to play a musical instrument by reading about the history of music. You must play the instrument. We felt that for our staff to make better use of technology, they needed hands on experience. In addition to supplying the computer, we also agreed there was a need to provide some over the shoulder human resource support as well.

Every-thing was progressing well until we (the central office "suits") were asked to meet with a small group of principals. We were taken aback when they told us they did not want the desk top computers! They claimed that if we really wanted the staff to become computer literate, they should have access to the computers 24/7, including evenings, weekends, and summer holidays. They asked us to consider providing lap tops rather than the desk top computers that would be anchored to their respective desks in the workplace. We thanked them for their delegation and retreated to an administrative huddle. We will get back to you!

THE CHICKEN COOP CEO

Looking back now, I can see how dangerously close I was to repeating my crucible at Ste. Anne Collegiate not that long ago. I was witnessing the central administrative staff begin to indulge in "confirmation bias." We started brainstorming all the reasons why giving out over 200 lap top computers would not be a good idea. Would we need extended insurance on the computers? What about loss or damage of the computers? What about information stored on the computers? Someone even went as far as to raise a concern that such a generous act as providing each teacher with a lap top computer could be perceived as tampering with the teachers' collective agreement.

> *All my training, experience and past failures helped inform a decision that would make a difference. I slept well that night .*

I asked our group of central office administrators (myself included) if we had more integrity as professionals and were more trustworthy than teachers and principals? Everyone said, of course not. Ah. But we all had our own lap top computers that we carried around with us. Long pause. Epiphany. If, as central office administrators, we could be trusted to take care of a lap top, why could we not trust the teachers and principals to do the same? In the end, we agreed that if we wanted the staff to get the most bang for the buck they needed to have 24/7 access to their computers. We decided to act on the advice of the principals and embark on a three-year plan to provide all teachers and principals with a lap top computer for their personal use. All my training, experience and past failures helped inform a decision that would make a difference. I slept well that night.

As we embarked on the project to supply the lap tops, we continued to take into account other important consideration of change management. First, we decided to try it with the few before recommending to the many. We had fifteen schools. We decided to embark on a three-year plan with five schools per year receiving the lap tops. Which schools? We did not want to dictate. Some schools were more prepared than others to get going in year one. We invited principals to apply to be equipped in the first year of implementation. This allowed the early adopters to shine. It allowed others to hang back and maybe focus on a more urgent issue in their respective schools in year one and two; in other words, prevent initiative overload for some.

In the first year seven schools applied to be equipped in year one. It was an interesting aspect of change theory to have to contact two principals and say, "thank you for your enthusiasm to embrace change, but you must wait one more year!" Both the real and perceived value of the initiative was firmly in place. Good idea. Good implementation. We had beat the odds.

Finally, how would we measure progress? We had hired an individual to conduct a pre-test of technological literacy of the staff in the Year One schools before the lap tops were distributed and post tested at the end of the first year. We collected solid data that demonstrated the increased literacy we were seeking.

No computers were lost or damaged in that first year.

Chapter 11 Key Takeaways

- People will support and attempt a change that is seen to be safe, possible, and valuable.

- A good idea needs a good implementation plan to succeed.

- Leaders must be open to being influenced to changing their minds in the face of new evidence.

CHAPTER 12 –
Time Management

"Give me six hours to chop down a tree and I will spend the first four sharpening the axe."
– Abraham Lincoln

A Short History of "Time Keeping"

Considering the length of man's existence on Earth, the concept of keeping precise time of day is a very recent phenomenon. For millennia, people have measured time based on the position of the sun; it was noon when the sun was the highest in the sky. Sun dials were used well into the Middle Ages, at which time mechanical clocks began to appear. Before that keeping track of time at night was done by observing the stars, burning candles or by measuring the amount of water that flowed through a small hole in one container into another.

With the advent of mechanical clocks, cities would set their town clock by measuring the position of the sun, but every city would be on a slightly different time. In the 1880's with the proliferation of train routes, towns along the train track had to standardize time to avoid train wrecks. It wasn't until 1918 that the Standards Time Act was officially adopted. And so, it started…the rigour with which people began to be a slave to the almighty clock.

Managing Time is a Myth

I don't want to get into a semantics argument, but really, we can not manage time. We can not speed it up or slow it down, except before quitting time on Friday. But we can manage ourselves and how we manage the same 168 hours we all get each week. I have my own list of seven approaches I use to get the most out of my 168 hours.

Seven Personal Management Tips

1. **"Eat the frog." – Don't procrastinate**

> *"If it is your job to eat a frog, it is best to do it first thing in the morning. And if it's your job to eat two frogs, it's best to eat the biggest frog first."*

It was the famous American author and humourist, Mark Twain, who said, "If it is your job to eat a frog, it is best to do it first thing in the morning. And if it's your job to eat two frogs, it's best to eat the biggest frog first." My Grandmother preached a similar approach to avoiding procrastination. She would tell me to make my bed right away when I got up in the morning and to get my chores done before I went out to play.

We all have things we don't want to do, but really, really need to do. It makes no sense to put it off. Get at right away in the morning when you are fresh and full of energy. Leave the things you want to do and don't need to do for later. At the end of the day if you have some things you want to do, but actually don't need to do, go for it then.

Procrastination occurs when we choose to engage in pleasurable short term activities rather than work on longer term projects which involve a deferral of gratification. In his book, *The Procrastination Equation*,

Piers Steel states, "proximity to temptation is one of the deadliest determinants of procrastination."[15] When you turn on your computer in the morning, what happens? You check email. Maybe you check for updates on Facebook, LinkedIn, or Twitter. How did the Winnipeg Jets do last night? Is Tiger Woods ready for a comeback? What will the weather be like on the weekend? There is a wide array of distractions that scream out: "The frog can wait!" While technology can help us be more efficient in our work, it can also present a compelling number of options that make distraction easy and pervasive.

2. **Don't handle a piece of paper more than twice (4 "D's").**

In my office, I used to maintain an in box and out box for print materials and other to do actions. I remember picking up certain pieces of paper several times then throwing them back in the in box only to pick them up and look at them again the next morning. Later, I tried to work with the maxim, "don't handle a piece of paper more than twice." I also practiced the four "D's":

    a   If it would only take a couple of minutes, **Do** it.

    b   If possible and appropriate, **Delegate** it.

    c   If it is important, I need to deal with it myself but don't have the time right away, **Defer** it (but no more than once).

    d   **Drop** it! Some fires go out on their own.

3. **For people that need to meet with you, book meetings around your schedule.**

Many people with good intentions don't understand the concept of an open-door policy. If there is an urgent and important issue to deal with, of course the door is open. However, important but not urgent items can wait so long as you have a plan to get to them in a reasonable amount of time. In SRSD we developed a management meeting system for the important but not urgent issues. We met twice a month as a management team. We kept an open agenda on a computer hard drive. Anyone could get an item on the agenda for the next team meeting and we would deal with the issue then.

4. **Take care of your health (including a nap at noon).**

I know that if I attend to three parts of my life, all of which are in my control I will come to work in condition to make the most effective use of my on-task time. You will remember from Chapter Eight that those three things are: sleep, nutrition, and exercise.

5. **Clean up your work station at the end of the day.**

You may have heard the saying that, "A tidy desk is the sign of a troubled mind!" Funny, but not true! How much time do people spend trying to find something on a cluttered desk? A must read on this topic is, *The Life-Changing Magic of Tidying Up*, by Marie Kondo. She proclaims, "The lives of those who tidy up thoroughly and completely, in a single shot, are without exception dramatically altered," and, "one of the magical effects of tidying is confidence in your decision-making capacity."[16]

Another way to keep our works space functional is to also tidy up our files. This is the electronic age. How many of us insist on keeping hard copies of certain files and documents that have been stored electronically? As a baby-boomer I can attest to the problem this is for me. Marie Kondo explains that the first step in tiding up is to discard objects. She goes on to explain that there are only two reasons to hold on to something. Firstly, if it touches your heart, or has sentimental value, keep it. As I mentioned earlier, I am an avid golfer. Note I said avid, not expert. After hundreds of rounds of golf, I scored my first hole in one in August of 2007 on the Hecla Golf Course. I have the Callaway golf ball proudly staged in a souvenir box in my office. No one is going to discard this memento; it touches my heart!

The second reason we cling to things is that we fear that we will need that object, file, piece of correspondence, etc. in the future. This does not explain why many of us have three of four filing cabinets full of correspondence from 1981. Discard!

6. **Manage the use of technology appropriately.**

    a Don't attempt to multitask for cognitive intense activities. Brain research has now concluded that multi-tasking is as false construct. Rene Marois, Department of Psychology, Vanderbilt University Research has offered neurological evidence that the brain cannot do two things at once. The term multitasking originated in the 1960's when computer operating systems were designed to share a single processor between several independent jobs. Multitasking is for machines, not people!

        We don't multitask; we switch task. Switch tasking lessens the efficient use of our time. When we switch task, it takes time to get back up to speed to resume the work where we left off.

        Don't confuse multitasking with background tasking. I like to listen to music when I go for a jog, but that is not multitasking and those two activities are not cognitively draining.

    b Turn off email/text notifications.

The average number of minutes an employee can devote to a project before being interrupted is only 11.[17]

The most common interruptions at work is the arrival of new email. Some estimates now suggest that email takes up as much as 40% of work life. Most people check email 40 – 50 times a day. Banishing email notification will make you about 10% more efficient…one month of productivity a year! Remember the earlier discussion around procrastination? What an immediate gratification it is to stop what we are doing to check who just emailed or texted messages. How many of those notifications need immediate attention?

c   Turn off devices – you don't need to be available 24/7

Just because technology makes it possible for you to be available 24/7 doesn't mean that you must be. Dr. Edward Hallowell, an expert in attention deficit disorder shared in a USA Today article, "A female patient asked me if I thought it was abnormal that her husband lays the BlackBerry on the bed when they make love." It seems to me we have a problem.

Why are some people firing off email messages at 4:00 AM? Are they up working at 4:00 AM every day, or are they trying to impress a supervisor of their diligence? Neither reason makes it an appropriate regular way of doing business. Remember we need 7-9 hours sleep a night.

As a leader, you can make it known when you will be available. Maybe you return emails before the end of a work day; not the minute they come in, unless there is an emergency to attend to.

7. **Use the Q2 planning method.**

I have saved my favorite, best personal management strategy for the last. The quadrant two planning method was popularized by Stephen Covey in his seminal book, *The Seven Habits of Highly Effective People*.[18] Covey created a matrix using the concepts of urgency and importance in how we choose to spend our time. It looks like this:

Personal Management Matrix	
Urgent/Important I ACTIVITIES: Crises Pressing problems Dead-line driven projects	Not Urgent/Important II ACTIVITIES: Relationship building Professional reading Planning Recreation
Urgent/Not Important III ACTIVITIES: Interruptions, some calls Some email Popular activities Another person's agenda	Not Urgent/Not Important IV ACTIVITIES: Trivia, "Busy Work" Some email Some phone calls Pleasant activities

This matrix clusters our daily activities into four categories:

1. Urgent and important
2. Not urgent and important
3. Urgent and not important
4. Not urgent not important.

I have given some examples of activities in each of the quadrants above.

You will notice that some email (maybe a lot!) is noted in the not important quadrants 3 and 4.

There are times when we must be working in quadrant one. The secret is to plan time to spend on activities in quadrant two; doing that which is not urgent but is very important. Let's take building positive relations as an example. As a CEO, I always found it important to get out of the office, visit the schools and other workplaces, to loiter with intent. The stronger the relations with employees, the greater the trust and the less likely that some of the relationship issues become important and urgent and end up being quadrant one issues. Do more in quadrant two; lessen the need to spend time in quadrant one putting out fires.

When I do workshops on the topic of personal time management, I like to ask two questions:

1. What one thing in Q2 could I do (that I am not doing right now; important but not urgent) that if I did on a regular basis would make a tremendous positive difference in my **personal** life?
2. What one thing in Q2 could I do (that I am not doing right now; important but not urgent) that if I did on a regular basis would make a tremendous positive difference in my **professional** life?

I then ask the workshop participants to make a personal commitment to work on the activities that they have identified. The commitment can come in the form of a "hope letter." Write down the intended activities, seal them in a self-addressed envelope which you entrust to a friend who will return the letter to you in one year. That type of activity tends to keep us honest on our hope of becoming a more effective person.

Chapter 12 Key Takeaways

- Monitor your use of technology; don't be the slave to a tool that is supposed to serve you, not the other way around.

- Multitasking cognitive intense activities is a myth.

- Plan non-urgent but important activities into your schedule.

CHAPTER 13 –
Planning and the Importance of Vision

"Everything should be made as simple as possible but no simpler."
– Albert Einstein

I like the quote above by Albert Einstein because it focuses on the most important element of planning: keep it simple.

I have shared earlier my first feeble attempts at system planning as the new Principal of LaBroquerie Elementary School back in the 1970's. I have had to learn, often the hard way, that an effective planning process does not reside in the responsibility of a single person and the bigger the stakes the more others need to be engaged in the process. While the leader can have a vision of what a successful organization should look like, if it is not a shared vision, it is of little value. It is the leader's responsibility to engage others. It is also the job of the leader to facilitate the discussion regarding the core ethical values and beliefs that will guide the actions that move the vision and mission into goals and concrete action plans.

Framework for Planning

Key Considerations in Strategic Planning

Consideration	Comment
"Plans are useless; planning is invaluable." – Peter Drucker	The process is as important as the outcome.
"The best plans are 'slim and sticky' not 'fat and forgettable.'" – Michael Fullan	It is important to limit goals to those things which matter most right now and will make the biggest difference.
Do you want to solve a problem or realize a vision about the best we can be?	The importance of a positive mindset and "appreciative inquiry."
People will support/do that which they believe to be safe possible and valuable.	The importance of involving people in decisions that affect them.
Actions are purposeful and focused rather than chaotic and haphazard.	Both vision and action are important.
Effective planning allows us to maximize resources.	We can always use more dollars.

The most complex and the most important duty of a leader is to begin the dialogue around shaping a vision for the organization. It is also the most difficult to get the support and agreement of others that this is where we want to go. A vision may start with one leader, but others must be willing to share the vision. Like everything else in the world, a vision starts in the mind.

Notwithstanding my annual struggles to get the Christmas tree lights to work, I think we can all agree that electricity is a good thing. Growing up, even though we lived in some bleak housing arrangements with no running water and wood burning heaters, we always had electricity in our home.

Thank you, Nikola Tesla, the inventor of the electric age. While not having been given the recognition he deserves, his inventions, patents and theoretical work led the way to modern alternating current electricity. Ok, where am I going with this? I am not an expert on the technical aspects of electricity or its application to the many inventions that changed the quality of life for humanity. What I did find interesting about the work of Tesla was his approach to the art and science of inventing.

It has been said that everything created by man in the physical world must first be created in the mind. So, it was that Tesla would not tinker with prototypes and the normal trial and error approach to inventing. He chooses instead to investigate his inventions in his imagination. He once stated, "I started by first picturing in my mind a direct-current machine, running it, and following the changing flow of the currents in the rotor. Then I would imagine an alternator (an AC generator) and investigate the processes taking place in a similar manner. Next, I would visualize systems comprising motors and generators and operate them in various ways. The images I saw were to me perfectly real and tangible."[19]

He created a totally completed functioning machine in his mind's vision and then created it as a final product in the physical world.

There are other types of visions that can lead to creations in the world that can have a positive effect on many people over long periods of time. You do not have to be an electrical engineer to be a visionary. I know of a proud small town hockey player, community member and leader who had a vision more than sixty-five years ago, that manifested into the physical world. That manifestation was an indoor community hockey rink and a public-spirited group of people known as "Le Club Sportif de LaBroquerie."

This small rural town situated in the South-East corner of Manitoba is known for its dairy farming, strong ties to its Franco-Manitoban founders and its hockey teams. I personally had the privilege of playing senior hockey in that town as well as coaching both minor level and senior level hockey. I was always aware of the proud tradition of the town's hockey history. It all started back in the 1948-1949 hockey season.

Indoor hockey rinks in Manitoba in the late 40's were few and far between. Certainly, there were no towns the size of LaBroquerie that had built one. The town itself had only about 50 homes, with the whole parish having about 200 families.

In 1948 a group of hearty sportsman founded the first LaBroquerie senior hockey team. They played in the Carillon Hockey League that first year. The other teams in the league were Grunthal, Otterburne and Niverville. The teams played on outdoor rinks. The LaBroquerie Sportsmen (later renamed the LaBroquerie Habs) best effort that first year was a 5-5 tie with Grunthal. The Sportsmen finished in last place.

In 1949-50 the LaBroquerie team again entered the Carillon League with teams from Grunthal, Niverville and Ste. Anne who replaced Otterburne.

This is when a vision was created.

> *The Vision: "If we win the cup this year, we will build an indoor arena."*

At the beginning of the season, team player and representative George Boily, proclaimed a vision that would have a profound positive effect on the Parish to this day. He said to his fellow teammates, "If we win the cup, we will build an indoor arena." At the time this seemed a bold and probably safe pronouncement given the team's record the previous year. Could this become a real-life creation like Tesla's AC motor?

At the end of the season Grunthal finished first in the league standings. Niverville and LaBroquerie, the second and third place teams played a best of three series to decide who would advance to the league final against Grunthal. LaBroquerie won the series two games to none with 1-0 and 4-0 victories. Could the sudden winning streak continue against the powerhouse Grunthal team in a best of five final?

> *When a person or an organization is clear about and dedicated to achieving a vision, the fates seem to conspire in their favour.*

When Grunthal won the first game 4-1, even the most loyal of LaBroquerie fans were prepared to say, even if we lose, it was a pretty good season; and we won't have to worry about building an indoor arena. However unlikely it may have seemed the Sportsmen won two of the next three games to force a fifth and deciding game in Grunthal. So far in the series the home team won both their games. With the fifth game back in Grunthal it seemed that victory, potentially so close, would not be attainable. It is strange that when a person or an organization is clear about and dedicated to achieving a vision, the fates seem to conspire in their favour.

It would not be until November 1, 1959 that Jacques Plante of the Montreal Canadians would wear a protective mask in a hockey game. In 1950, the unfortunate Grunthal goalie certainly was not wearing one when he was hit squarely between the eyes early in the first period of that final and fateful fifth and deciding game. Grunthal had no back up goalie. His eyes were swollen and it was later reported that he suffered blackouts periodically during the game. Despite the Grunthal goalies valiant effort to play on, LaBroquerie promptly scored four unanswered goals and went on to a 5-2 victory and were proud recipients of the Leagues Championship trophy, the Prefontaine Cup.

The rest is history as they say and you can look it up! The Sportsmen started the realization of George Boily's vision of building an indoor arena.

It would take almost two and one half years for the project to be completed. It is a truly inspiring testimonial to community spirit and volunteerism that the project even got started much less completed. Volunteers literally went into the bush over the winter to cut the trees to make the lumber for the arena. Volunteers provided most of the labour. Fund raising, donations and grants contributed to financing. The official organization that was created and provided project oversight was the Club Sportif, a volunteer organization that continues to function to this day.

The official opening of the arena took place January 28, 1953. At the annual general meeting of the Club Sportif on April 22, 1953 it was announced that it had cost $5000 to build the arena.

It would be impossible to calculate the invaluable contribution that original hockey rink and the two replacements that followed has had on not only the community of LaBroquerie, but also the inspiration it provided for surrounding communities to follow. Thousands of children and adults have benefited and continue to benefit from the vision of a small-town hockey team and one hockey player, George Boily who had the vision and the courage to say, "If we win the cup we will build an arena!"

In my own role as a CEO for fourteen years in the public education system, and eight subsequent years working with organizations, I have come to understand the critical importance of having a vision. My experience has been that this important first step in planning is often missing or not clearly articulated. While it might not appear that way, visioning is hard work.

As a leader, what is your vision for the system or company you work for? How clear is it in your mind and in your heart? What is it that you want to see manifested into the physical world and what are you going to do to help it materialize?

Chapter 13 Key Takeaways

- Any organization's strategic plan must begin with a vision for the organization: what will a successful organization look like? It is the leaders job to lead that discussion.

- Involve the expertise of everyone in the system when establishing vision.

EPILOGUE –
My Story Revisited: Poverty, Continuous Learning, and Purpose

"We shall not cease from exploration, and the end of all our exploring will be to arrive where we started and know the place for the first time."
– T. S. Eliot

While it is nearing completion, the final chapter of my life story is not over. However, as I take this opportunity to look back and reflect on my journey so far, and with that longitudinal perspective in mind, I will make some observations about where I have come from, where I am now, and what yet lies ahead. Remember, it is our life story, with its crucibles along the way and those significant influencers that defines our leadership. Add to that the recognition of the importance of continuous learning and having a reason to get up in the morning, there might even be more chapters yet to write.

Growing up in Poverty

> *Poverty is not found in our DNA. There is no gene for poverty.*

I began my story by sharing some of the issues that come with growing up in poverty. You can not escape your past, nor should you try. Where you come from is what makes you unique. I have come to understand that poverty is not found in our DNA. There is no gene for poverty. Poverty is an external condition that confronts millions of people around the world every day. Poverty was a condition that confronted the Seidler children, including myself, while we were growing up. We can choose to take a positive view to external conditions but it does not hurt to have some help along the way. The support of my Mother, my Grandparents and many other influential people in my life prepared me to overcome the drawbacks that are associated with growing up in poverty. As I have explained earlier I also believe that there are tipping points, or crucibles that shape our lives.

In 2014, a Gallup Poll was conducted of American college graduates who had been in the workplace for five years. The graduates were asked what were the factors in their education that mattered the most in their future success in work and in life. What was revealed was not what college they attended, but rather *how* they got their education that contributed to their success. Two experiences stood out. I call them the significant influencer factors.

The more than two million workers, students and employers reported that successful students had one or more teachers during their schooling and one or more mentors in the workplace that took a real interest in them. The study concluded that the most engaged employees consistently attributed their success in life and the workplace to having had a teacher or mentor, who cared about them as a person. Yes. That is right. Something as inspirationally simple as having someone who genuinely cares about you as a person!

The most significant influencer, other than immediate family, in my early life, in my school years, was Mr. Lepage. His intervention during my K – Grade 12 public education experience was a major turning point in my life; it has made all the difference. Public education is the one social institution that can change the fortunes of a family in one generation. I know this to be true because it happened to me. In the latter stages of my life story, Mr. Jean Suszko was my mentor, another significant influencer. Like Mr. Lepage, he saw something in me that gave him the confidence to support my move up the succession board.

So, with the right attitude, some perseverance, the help of significant influencers, and some timely crucibles, no matter what kind of a hand we are dealt with early in life, it is possible to be all in and win the pot. And, it helps to be lucky.

Continuous Learning and Personal Growth

While I have made references to the importance of continuous learning throughout earlier chapters, I would like to revisit this critical attribute of great leaders. Continuous learning is a mindset; a belief system; maybe even a hunger. You must want to learn and grow. If anything, as we age, the desire to learn and grow should be stronger than ever. It keeps us young, and we are running out of time. Once we graduate from University, our personal growth must become self-directed. We should want to learn and grow not to meet some external requirement such as passing an exam or retaining a professional designation. While I still enjoy attending workshops and presentations by others, my main source of growth continues to be the old fashion way. I read a lot! And the more I read, the more I learn, the more connections I find between the various areas of study.

There has never been a time in history when it has been more important to embrace the concept of continuous learning. We are living in a time of exponential change. My most recent personal continuous learning initiative was to read the new book out by Thomas L. Friedman, *Thank You for Being Late*. In his book, he gives a great example to help us understand this concept of rapid change that is happening with technology. It reminded me again that we are living in times of exponential change, the age of acceleration.

The first micro processing chip, the 4004 Microchip, went into production in 1971. The most recent Intel microchip update came this year, in 2016. Compared to the original 4004 chip, the 2016 Intel microchip provides 3,500 times more performance capability, is 90,000 times more energy efficient and costs 60,000 times less than that first chip back in 1971. It is hard for the average mind, like mine, to understand what this really means in terms of understanding exponential change. The concept of exponential change as it applies to technology has been best defined by Moore's Law that predicted the power of microchips would double roughly every two years. He made that prediction in 1965.

Suppose as a starting point in 1971, the year the 4004 microchip was produced, we considered a Volkswagen Beetle car. What would happen if the same exponential rate of change that has happened with the improvements in microchips had also happened with the Volkswagen? This is what would have happened. A 2016 Volkswagen would be able to travel at a speed of 300,000 miles per hour, would require one gallon of gas to travel 1 million miles, and would cost four cents!

Friedman goes on to explain that the rate of change is accelerating. 1000 years ago, it took about one hundred years for an innovation or change to make its way into the mainstream society. An example cited was the invention of the long bow.

100 years ago, it only took about 25 – 30 years for an innovation or change to impact on society; think of the airplane or automobile.

In 2016, similar impactful inventions take only 5 – 7 years to become part of mainstream society. The first smartphone (iPhone) was unveiled in 2007, lest we forget, and how many of us now own and use one?

The problem that Friedman identifies is that the ability of people to adapt is not keeping up with the accelerating pace if change. "When fast gets really fast, being slower to adapt makes you really slow – and ***disoriented***. When the pace of change gets this fast, the only way to retain a lifelong working capacity is to engage in lifelong learning."[20]

I recently bought a hard copy of the manual for my iPhone. It has over 600 pages of text to help a person understand how to use the device and all its functions. Sorry, but I am "disoriented!" I just get accustomed to Windows 7 and now I must learn how to use Windows 10. And it does not recognize my printer. Yes, I feel disoriented.

While for some, learning and growth may slow down as we age, it never ends, nor should it. If anything, with the advantage of a lifetime of learning and experience, our growth should be even more profound. But, we must keep at it. In life, there will be lessons. Lessons are repeated until learned, and learning never ends. Lifelong learning is no longer a platitude; it is a necessity.

As residents of the new "age of acceleration," we will need to expand the requirements of a successful leader. The twenty-first century leader will continue to be someone who helps individuals and organizations achieve goals. But, to do that they will have to help others face the new reality of accelerated change and assist them in making change more rapidly.

Purpose – Finding Your "ikigai"

My final thoughts return to the importance of purpose. We can find purpose in all aspects of our lives. Our commitment to family and friends; our involvement in community activities and volunteerism. And of course, it is important to find purpose and meaning in our work. Like the centenarians of Okinawa, we need to be careful in how we define retirement.

Entering full retirement can be bad for your health. Studies of this life change indicate that complete retirement leads to increases in difficulty in physical mobility, increases in illness conditions and a decline in mental health. Not a rosy picture.

When I stopped working as a Superintendent/CEO in 2008 at the age of 59, I was grateful and appreciative of the many social events that were held to wish me well as I rode off into the sunset. However, at times I felt like I was hearing a eulogy better left for when I died. I personally did not feel I was retiring but rather transitioning into another stage of my life. As a matter of fact, along with my partner Odette, I was well along the way to establishing our company, ROAR Leadership Consultants. My contract with Seine River School Division ended on August 31, 2008. My contract to take on the services as the Executive Director of the Manitoba Association of School Business Officials started September 1, 2008.

Please don't think that I am feeling sorry for myself here. Quite the contrary, I feel I have been lucky in my life. My life story, my internal narrative, is one of redemption, to use the phrase coined by Amy Cuddy. The challenges and crucibles that I have experienced have served to improve my attitude and help me gain wisdom, as limited as that might be!

Although I would still have a work schedule in my new position as the Executive Director of MASBO in 2008, it was a lighter one and provided for a great deal of autonomy. I performed those duties, along with other consultant work, until the end of August 2016. I will slow down some more, but I remain very committed to continuing with contract work that will allow me to follow my passion and my purpose in my work life: to support public education and to realize my personal mission of: "Learn-Grow-Share." Another transition is in progress. I wonder what the next one will look like? I will probably get lucky again!

This is what I wish for you. Be clear about your purpose in life. What is your "ikigai?" What is your reason to jump out of bed in the morning, ready and even excited to get to the work that you love and that provides meaning in your life? If you are not quite there yet, please keep looking. Life is short enough. Don't waste it on something that drains your emotional, mental and physical energy with nothing to show in return. If you have not yet found it, your "ikigai" is waiting to be discovered.

ENDNOTES

1. *Man's Search for Meaning*, Viktor E. Frankl, Washington Square Press, 1959, PP. 16-17

2. *Presence*, Amy Cuddy, Little Brown, 2015, P.89

3. *Outliers*, Malcolm Gladwell, Little Brown, 2008, PP. 39-40

4. *Working with Emotional Intelligences*, Daniel Goleman, Bantam Books, 1998, P. 19

5. *Working with Emotional Intelligences*, Daniel Goleman, Bantam Books, 1998, P. 34

6. http://en.wikipedia.org/wiki/Jean_Chastel

7. *The Feeling of What Happens*, Antonio Damasio, New York: Harcourt Press, 1999

8. *The No Asshole Rule*, Robert I. Sutton, Warner Business Books, 2007, PP. 71-72

9. *Good to Great*, Jim Collins, Harper Business, 2001

10. *Presence: Bringing your Boldest Self to your Biggest Challenges*, Amy Cuddy, Little Brown, 2015, PP. 51-52

11. *A Whole New Mind*, Daniel H. Pink, 2005, Riverhead Books

12. *Sleeping Your Way to the Top*, Terry Cralle, W. David Brown, William Cane, Sterling, 2016, PP. 4-5

13 *Get Rid of the Performance Review*, Samuel Culbert, Business Plus, 2010, P.1

14 *Drive*, Daniel H. Pink, Riverhead Books, 2009, P. 218

15 *The Procrastination Equation*, Piers Steel, Random House Canada, 2010. P. 64

16 *The Life Changing Magic of Tidying Up*, Marie Kondo, Ten Speed Press, 2014, P. 178

17 *The Myth of Multitasking*, Dave Crenshaw, Jossey-Bass, 2008, P. 16

18 *The Seven Habits of Highly Effective People*, Stephen R. Covey, Simon and Schuster, 1989

19 Nikola Tesla, *"My Inventions" in Electrical Experiments Magazine*, May-October Ed., 1919

20 *Thank You for Being Late*, Thomas L. Friedman, Farrar, Straus and Giroux, PP. 32,33

ACKNOWLEDGEMENTS

Just as I had many "significant influencers" along my leadership development path, I had many people who helped get my book to the final publishing stage. Thank you to all the friends and professional associates who were kind enough to share their opinions of my work along the way.

As a first-time author, I could not have succeeded in my publishing efforts without the professional assistance of the great people at Friesen Press. Thanks to Ellie Moller who was my main point of contact and patiently and expertly guided me thought the various stages of getting a book ready for printing.

Finally, thanks to my partner in life, business and golf, Odette, for being both my fiercest critic and my most loyal supporter.

CPSIA information can be obtained
at www.ICGtesting.com
Printed in the USA
LVOW05s1931070917
547883LV00007B/11/P